Dramascripts

The Hound of the Baskervilles

SIR ARTHUR CONAN DOYLE

Adapted by
John O'Connor

Nelson

Nelson Thornes Ltd.
Delta Place
27 Bath Road
CHELTENHAM
GL53 7TH
United Kingdom

ıⓉⱣ® Thomas Nelson is an International Thomson Company
ıⓉⱣ® is used under licence

The Hound of the Baskervilles – the script
© John O'Connor 1998
The right of John O'Connor to be identified as author of this play has been asserted by
John O'Connor in accordance with Copyright, Design and Patents Act 1988.

Introduction, activities and explanatory notes
© Thomas Nelson 1998

Designed and produced by Bender Richardson White
Typesetting by Malcolm Smythe
Cover illustration by Dave Grimwood
Black and white illustrations by John James
Printed by Multivista Global Ltd

This edition published by Thomas Nelson & Sons Ltd 1998
ISBN 978 - 0 - 17 - 432557 - 4
9   8   7
09

CONTENTS

SERIES EDITOR'S INTRODUCTION

Dramascripts is an exciting series of plays especially chosen for students in the lower and middle years of secondary school. The titles range from the best in modern writing to adaptations of classic texts such as *A Christmas Carol* and *Silas Marner*.

Dramascripts can be read or acted purely for the enjoyment and stimulation that they provide; however, each play in the series also offers all the support that pupils need in working with the text in the classroom:

- **Introduction** – this offers important background information and explains something about the ways in which the play came to be written.
- **Script** – this is clearly set out in ways that make the play easy to handle in the classroom.
- **Notes** explain references that pupils might not understand, and language points that are not obvious.
- **Activities** – at the end of scenes, acts or sections – give pupils the opportunity to explore the play more fully. Types of activity include: discussion, writing, hot-seating, improvisation, acting, freeze-framing, story-boarding and artwork.
- **Looking Back at the Play** – this section has further activities for more extended work on the play as a whole with emphasis on characters, plots, themes and language.

SET AND MUSIC

The set and the music are designed to create a fluent, unbroken performance.

SET

The acting space should be square with an exit at each corner. Audience sit on three sides, the fourth being curtained off (and concealing a screen, on to which the images of the hound are back-projected towards the end of the play).

If the curtain is thought to be along the north side of the space, the north-west corner will contain a minimalist representation of Holmes's study in Act 1, and Baskerville Hall in Act 2. The opposite (south-east) corner will contain flooring (hillocks, rocks, etc.) to represent the moor in Act 2.

Many exterior locations are established by sound-effects only (e.g. the traffic in Baker Street, changing into the clatter of type-writers as the characters enter the District Messengers' Office).

Any props will be brought on by characters, and furniture set in place during the brief black-outs.

MUSIC

The solo violin heard at the beginning (which turns out to be played by Holmes) provides music throughout. It is used to add to the tension and atmosphere (for example, when Watson and Sir Henry are following Barrymore through the house at night), and at every scene-change marked by a black-out.

Ideally the music should be live, but there are many appropriate recordings which can be used.

THE CHARACTERS

FROM LONDON:

SHERLOCK HOLMES

DR WATSON

BOOT-BOY
⎫
MANAGER
⎭ in the Northumberland Hotel

MR POTTER   of the District Messengers' Office

STATION PORTER

INSPECTOR LESTRADE   from Scotland Yard

Voice of a Hansom cab driver

FROM CANADA:

SIR HENRY BASKERVILLE   the new owner of Baskerville Hall

FROM DARTMOOR:

DR JAMES MORTIMER   a country doctor

SIR CHARLES BASKERVILLE   Sir Henry's uncle

BARRYMORE   Butler at Baskerville Hall

MRS BARRYMORE   his wife

STAPLETON
⎫
BERYL STAPLETON
⎭ of Merripit House

SELDEN   an escaped convict

LAURA LYONS   of Coombe Tracey

A servant in Baskerville Hall

THE HOUND OF THE BASKERVILLES
ACT 1 ❖ *SCENE 1*

A s the houselights dim to blackout, a solo violin is heard, playing something loud, discordant and dramatic. After a few bars, the music changes: the violin plays more quietly; but its mood becomes one of tension and foreboding.

It stops, and the silence is broken by a terrifying sound: the baying of a monstrous hound.

The violin strikes up again, dramatic as before, and a single spot comes up centre stage, into which staggers an elderly man, clearly frightened out of his wits. He stares frantically around him, trying to determine the source of the unearthly sound, then turns towards an exit. But, before he reaches it, there is an even louder baying than before. He spins round, stares ahead of him, and his eyes widen, registering an indescribable terror. Slowly he backs away, shaking his head in disbelief. Then, clutching his heart, he screams and falls to the ground, dead.

There is a sudden blackout and the violin reaches a crescendo of drama and agitation, during which . . .

a solo violin *One of Sherlock Holmes's favourite pastimes is playing the violin.*

a crescendo of drama and agitation *The music gets louder and louder and at the same time more dramatic and disturbed.*

ACT 1 ❖ SCENE 2

. . . the lights come up on a different part of the stage to reveal the source of the dramatic music: a violinist whom we are about to identify as SHERLOCK HOLMES.

A basic set indicates that we are in his apartment, 221B Baker Street. HOLMES has his back to most of the audience, but his companion, DR WATSON, faces outward. From his expression, we gather that he is not altogether appreciative of HOLMES'S playing, but is diverting himself by close examination of a walking-stick.

Abruptly, the playing ends and, without turning round, Holmes speaks.

HOLMES   Well, Watson, what do you make of it?

WATSON   How did you know what I was doing? I believe you have   1
eyes in the back of your head.

HOLMES   *(Depositing his violin.)* I
have, at least, a well
polished, silver-plated
coffee-pot in front of
me. But tell me,
Watson, what do you
make of our visitor's
stick? Since we have   10
been so unfortunate as
to miss him and have
no notion of his
errand, this accidental
souvenir becomes of
importance. Let me
hear you reconstruct
the man by an
examination of it.

WATSON   *(Clearly summoning all his wits.)* I think . . . I think that   20

Dr Mortimer is a successful elderly medical man, well-esteemed, since those who know him give him this mark of their appreciation.

HOLMES Good! Excellent!

WATSON *(Gaining in confidence.)* I think also that the probability is in favour of his being a country practitioner who does a great deal of his visiting on foot.

HOLMES Why so?

WATSON Because this stick, although originally a very handsome one, has been so knocked about that I can hardly imagine a town doctor carrying it. The thick iron ferrule is worn down, so it is evident that he has done a great amount of walking with it.

30

HOLMES Perfectly sound!

WATSON *(Now really in his stride, reading an inscription.)* And then again there is the 'Friends of the CCH'. I should guess that to be the Something-or-other Hunt, the local fox-hunt, to whom he has possibly given some surgical assistance, and which has made him a small presentation in return.

HOLMES *(Throwing himself into an armchair.)* Really, Watson, you excel yourself! I am bound to say that, in all the accounts which you have been so good as to give of my own small achievements, you have habitually underrated your own abilities. You are a constant source of stimulation to me. I confess, my dear fellow, that I am very much in your debt.

40

WATSON *(Clearly delighted at this rare praise.)* Well, Holmes, I can only say that I am pleased to have so far mastered your system of deduction, as to earn your approval. I sometimes think –

---

 ferrule *A metal ring used to strengthen the end of a stick.*

	But he breaks off as HOLMES, leaping up from his seat, snatches the stick from him and takes it to the window. 50
HOLMES	*(Examining the stick very cursorily.)* Interesting, though elementary. *(He throws the stick back to WATSON and returns to his chair.)* There are certainly one or two indications upon it. It gives us the basis for several deductions.
WATSON	*(Assuming an air of self-importance.)* Has anything escaped me? I trust that there is nothing of consequence that I have overlooked?
HOLMES	I am afraid, dear Watson, that most of your conclusions were erroneous. When I said that you stimulated me, I meant, to be frank, that in noting your mistakes, I was 60 occasionally guided towards the truth. Not that you are entirely wrong in this instance. The man is certainly a country practitioner. And he walks a good deal.
WATSON	*(Defensively.)* Then I was right.
HOLMES	To that extent.
WATSON	*(A distinct note of disappointment in his voice.)* But that was all?
HOLMES	No, no, my dear Watson, not all – by no means all. But I would suggest that a presentation to a doctor is more likely to come from a hospital than a hunt; and that, when the 70 initials 'CC' are placed before that hospital, the words Charing Cross very naturally suggest themselves.
WATSON	*(A little grudgingly.)* You may be right.
HOLMES	The probability lies in that direction. And this supposition gives us a fresh basis from which to start our construction of this unknown visitor.

   erroneous *'mistaken'*

WATSON	Well, then, supposing that CCH does stand for Charing Cross Hospital, what further inferences may we draw?
HOLMES	Do none suggest themselves? You know my methods. Apply them!

80

WATSON	I can only think of the obvious conclusion that the man has practised in town before going to the country.
HOLMES	I think we might venture a little further than that. Is it stretching things too far, for example, to suggest that the presentation of the stick was made on the occasion of some kind of change of circumstances?
WATSON	It certainly seems probable.
HOLMES	For example, when the young house doctor left the hospital to take up a post in the country? And he left only five years ago – the date is on the stick. So your grave, middle-aged family practitioner vanishes into thin air, my dear Watson, and there emerges a young fellow under thirty, amiable, unambitious, absent-minded, and a possessor of a favourite dog, which I should describe as being larger than a terrier and smaller than a mastiff.

90

WATSON stands amazed for a second and then bursts into laughter.

WATSON	As to the latter part, I have no means of checking you. But at least . . . *(He reaches down a book from the shelves.)* . . . At least we can find out a few particulars about the man's age and professional career. Let me see . . . Ah, yes, this must be our man. *(Reading.)* 'Mortimer, James, MRCS, 1882, Grimpen, Dartmoor, Devon. House surgeon from 1882 to 1884 at Charing – ahem – Charing Cross Hospital. Winner

100

?

Charing Cross Hospital *A major hospital in London.*

amiable *'pleasant and friendly'*

MRCS *Member of the Royal College of Surgeons*

---

of . . . et cetera . . . Doctor for the parishes of Grimpen, Thorsley and High Barrow.'

HOLMES *(Smiling mischievously.)* No mention of the local hunt, Watson. But a country doctor, as you astutely observed. As to the adjectives, I said, if I remember rightly, amiable, unambitious and absent-minded. It is my experience that it 110 is only an amiable man who receives presentations of this kind, only an unambitious one who abandons a London career for the country, and only an absent-minded one who leaves his stick and not his visiting-card after waiting for an hour in your room.

WATSON And the dog?

HOLMES *(Standing and walking to the window.)* Has been in the habit of carrying this stick behind his master. By the size of the teeth-marks, I should say it might have been – *(As he looks out.)* Yes, by Jove! It is a curly-haired spaniel! 120

WATSON My dear fellow, how can you possibly be so sure of that?

HOLMES For the simple reason that I see the dog itself on our very doorstep – *(The doorbell rings.)* And there is the ring of its owner. Now is the dramatic moment of fate, Watson, when you hear a step upon the stair which is walking into your life, and you know not whether for good or ill. What does Dr James Mortimer, the man of science, ask of Sherlock Holmes, the specialist in crime? *(There is a knock.)* Come in!

DR MORTIMER enters. He is tall, untidily dressed and good-natured. 130

MORTIMER *(Spying his walking stick.)* My stick! I am so very glad. I was not sure whether I had left it here or in the Shipping Office.

Grimpen, Dartmoor *Although Grimpen is a fictitious village, Dartmoor is an actual area of wild moorland in Devon.*

astutely *'shrewdly'; 'cleverly and perceptively'*

	I would not lose that stick for the world.	
HOLMES	A presentation, I see.	
MORTIMER	Yes, sir.	
HOLMES	From Charing Cross hospital?	
MORTIMER	From one or two friends there, on the occasion of my marriage.	
HOLMES	*(Shaking his head.)* Dear, dear, that's bad!	
MORTIMER	*(Mildly astonished.)* Why was it bad?	140
HOLMES	Only that you have disarranged our little deductions. Never mind. *(Standing and offering his hand.)* Dr James Mortimer?	
MORTIMER	Yes, sir. And I presume it is Mr Sherlock Holmes whom I am addressing and not – ?	
HOLMES	No, this is my friend, Doctor Watson.	
MORTIMER	Glad to meet you, sir. I have heard your name mentioned in connection with your friend. *(WATSON nods politely.)*	
HOLMES	And the purpose of your visit?	
MORTIMER	*(His expression suddenly becomes troubled.)* I came to you, Mr Holmes, because I recognise that I am myself an unpractical man, and because I am suddenly confronted with a most serious and extraordinary problem. *(He reaches into his coat pocket.)* I have in my pocket a manuscript.	150
HOLMES	I observed it as you entered the room.	
MORTIMER	It is an old manuscript.	
HOLMES	Early eighteenth century, unless it is a forgery. *(Observing MORTIMER'S surprise.)* You have been presenting an inch or two of it to my examination all the time you have been talking. I put it at 1730.	
MORTIMER	The exact date is 1742. *(Carefully opening the paper.)* This family paper was committed to my care by Sir Charles	160

Baskerville, whose sudden and tragic death some three months ago created so much excitement in Devonshire. I may say that I was his personal friend as well as his medical attendant. He was a strong-minded man, sir, shrewd, practical and unimaginative as I am myself. Yet he took this document very seriously, and his mind was prepared for just such an end as did eventually overtake him.

HOLMES   *(Taking the paper from DR MORTIMER.)* 'Baskerville Hall . . . 1740.' It appears to be a statement of some sort.   170

MORTIMER   Yes, it is an account of a certain legend which runs in the Baskerville family.

HOLMES   But I understand it is something more modern and practical on which you want to consult me?

MORTIMER   Most modern. A most practical, pressing matter which must be decided within twenty-four hours. But the manuscript is short and is intimately connected with the affair. With your permission I will read it to you.

HOLMES   Pray do not trouble yourself. I have looked through it as you were speaking. *(To WATSON.)* The manuscript tells of a   180
curse on the Baskerville family, Watson. It seems that a wicked ancestor, Sir Hugo, had decided to set his hounds on some innocent country girl who had rejected his corrupt advances. She died in the chase, but the evil Sir Hugo was himself pursued by some spectre – *(He looks back at the manuscript and reads.)* '. . .a foul thing, a great, black beast, shaped like a hound, yet larger than any hound that ever mortal eye has rested upon. And even as they looked, the thing tore the throat out of Hugo Baskerville . . .'.

MORTIMER   And many of the family have since come to sudden and   190
bloody ends. The manuscript tells of the punishment of providence carrying on into the third and fourth generations, as it says in the Bible. It also warns members of the family not to cross the moor in –

HOLMES	*(Interrupting him, reading from the manuscript, dramatically.)* '– In those dark hours when the powers of evil are exalted.'
MORTIMER	Do you find it interesting?
HOLMES	To a collector of fairy tales.
MORTIMER	*(Taking a folded newspaper from his pocket.)* In that case, Mr Holmes, I will give you something a little more recent. This is the Devon County Chronicle of June the 14th of this year. It is a short account of the facts elicited at the death of Sir Charles Baskerville. It begins with an account of the good works for which Sir Charles was known throughout the county, and then refers to his health, which had never been good – *(To WATSON.)* he had a weak heart and bouts of nervous depression.
WATSON	He talked to you about his depression?
MORTIMER	*(Becomes more troubled and thoughtful, as he recalls his friend's distraction.)* Many times. One occasion I recall most vividly.

200

210

The lights come up on the opposite corner of the stage to reveal the figure whose death was portrayed at the beginning – SIR CHARLES BASKERVILLE – while the lights dim on WATSON and HOLMES, who is now reading the article. SIR CHARLES has plainly been walking – he wears a cape and carries a stick – and the distant sound of birdsong can be heard. He is joined by MORTIMER, who approaches him from across the stage.

SIR CHARLES	This legend haunts me, Mortimer. Incredible as it may seem to you, I am convinced that some dreadful fate overhangs

the punishment of providence *The idea that heavenly powers would punish you if you committed some wrong-doing.*

the third and fourth generations, as it says in the Bible *In the Bible (Exodus, chapter 20), God warns that a whole family might be punished for one person's sins, right down to the grand-children and great-grandchildren.*

exalted *'raised up' 'at their most powerful'*

	my family – and you have to admit that the records of my ancestors' deaths are not encouraging.	220
MORTIMER	Many of our oldest families have an unhappy history of violent deaths, Sir Charles –	
SIR CHARLES	No, it's more than that. It's as though – *(Suddenly his arm jerks out, pointing over MORTIMER'S shoulder.)* Look! Look there! What do you see? What is it?	
MORTIMER	A calf, I think. A large, black calf. What it's doing on the moor, I can't imagine. I suppose – Sir Charles?	
	SIR CHARLES'S eyes are tight shut, he is clutching his chest and swaying slightly.	230
SIR CHARLES	*(Recovering enough to speak.)* Tell me, Mortimer, when you are called out at night and have to visit some poor wretch who lives on the moor, do you ever see . . . any strange creature . . . or hear perhaps . . . a hound baying?	
MORTIMER	Let me take you back to the Hall, Sir Charles. *(Leading him off.)* I will ask Barrymore to set in a good fire and then I recommend an early night.	
	The lights cross-fade to show HOLMES coming to the end of the article.	
HOLMES	'And his body was found at the end of the alley of yew trees, leading from the Hall. There were no marks of violence upon him, but he lay on his face, his arms out, his fingers dug into the ground . . .'	240
	As HOLMES reads, the lights come up once again on MORTIMER. He is examining the body of SIR CHARLES as it lies in the position that HOLMES describes.	
	'. . . and his features convulsed with some strong emotion, to such an extent that Dr Mortimer, his close friend and medical attendant, could scarcely swear to his identity . . .'	
	MORTIMER looks up from his examination of the body and	250

carefully checks the surrounding ground, muttering to himself.

MORTIMER	My footprints here . . . And these are Sir Charles's . . . On tip-toe? . . . What's this? Cigar ash. But nothing else, except – *(He stands still for a second, looking at the ground some yards ahead of him, then slowly approaches . . .)*

Lights come down on the body and up on HOLMES'S study. MORTIMER leaves the Dartmoor scene and returns to HOLMES and WATSON.

HOLMES	Footprints?	
MORTIMER	Footprints.	260
HOLMES	A man's or a woman's?	
MORTIMER	*(Looking strangely, first at WATSON, then HOLMES, his voice sinks almost to a whisper.)* Mr Holmes, they were the footprints of a gigantic hound!	

Slow fade to black-out.

ARTWORK: There have been several screen versions of this story. Imagine that you are filming your own. Storyboard scene 1, drawing four key frames. The first frame might look like this:

Write notes on what the viewer will hear (e.g. the wind blowing in the trees, an owl hooting).

Sketch what the viewer will see.

Write what the camera is doing (e.g. ground-level shot of Sir Charles lying dead, and Dr Mortimer kneeling over him; Baskervill Hall in the background).

WRITING: Look back at the conversation between Holmes and Watson about the cane that has been left behind. Write a scene of play script dialogue in which the two have a similar discussion about a different object that someone has left in Holmes's study (such as an old book, a hat or an empty bag).

WRITING: On pages 8 and 9, Holmes reads out some phrases from the old manuscript about the violent death of Sir Hugo. Write the full story of the wicked Sir Hugo, either in your own words or as it might appear in the old manuscript.

DISCUSSION: As a class, discuss what these opening scenes reveal about Holmes and Watson. What are they each like as individuals, and what have you learned about their friendship?

ACTING: In groups of four, act out Scene 2, from the point where Mortimer brings out the newspaper cutting about Sir Charles's death. Plan carefully how the scene should be staged.

DISCUSSION: Is there really a monstrous hound on the moor? If so, is it real ('material') or ghostly ('spectral')? As a class, discuss all the evidence presented so far which leads you to decide one way or the other.

ACT 1 ❖ SCENE 3

Early the following morning. A room in the Northumberland Hotel, London. The occupant is clearly in a bad temper: he is not yet fully dressed, still in his braces, and is striding about with one boot in his hand. As the scene opens, he goes to the exit and shouts out. He has a Canadian accent.

SIR HENRY	Boots! Boot-boy! Boots!	1
	The boy hurries in, scared.	
BOOTS	Yes, sir?	
SIR HENRY	Now, young feller, I don't know that much about British customs yet, but I hope that to lose one of your boots is not part of the ordinary routine of life over here?	
BOOTS	No, sir.	
SIR HENRY	Then where in tarnation is it?	
BOOTS	I don't know, sir. I – I'll look on the other floors. I'll find it, sir, I promise –	10
	The hotel manager enters, a small balding man, extremely flustered by the sound of an honoured guest in a bad mood.	
MANAGER	Is there a problem, Sir Henry?	
SIR HENRY	You bet there is. I left a pair of boots out last night to be cleaned. This morning one of the pair is missing.	

Boots! *It was the boot-boy's job to collect all the boots and shoes left outside people's bedroom doors overnight and have them cleaned by morning.*

tarnation *A polite form of 'damnation': 'Where the hell is it?'.*

MANAGER   I assure you it will be found, Sir Henry. There must be some simple explanation. *(He turns to the whimpering boot-boy and hisses.)* Get out and find it! *(Then back to SIR HENRY, with an ingratiating smile.)* I shall supervise the search personally, Sir. *(He bows, starts to leave, and then turns, remembering the reason for his visit.)* Oh, this arrived in this morning's post, Sir Henry *(handing him a letter).*   **20**

He leaves and SIR HENRY begins to open the letter, muttering to himself as he does so.

SIR HENRY   Weird. Who knows I'm here? . . . *(He opens the letter and reads.)* 'As you value your life or your reason, keep away from the Moor.' *(He looks back to question the manager, but he has gone and, after reading the paper once more, repeats to himself:)* '. . . your life or your *reason* . . .'?

Cross-fade to . . .   **30**

?   ingratiating *'over-friendly and polite' 'smarmy'*

ACT 1 ❖ SCENE 4

221B Baker Street. HOLMES and WATSON are finishing breakfast. HOLMES is drinking coffee; WATSON is leafing through papers, scattered across the breakfast table.

HOLMES	There are many sheep-dogs on the moor, Watson.	1
WATSON	Yes, but he claims these prints were enormous. And we need to account for the fact that, before this terrible event occurred, several people had seen a creature upon the moor which corresponds with this Baskerville demon, and which could not possibly be any animal known to science. They all agreed that it was – *(reaching for a sheet of paper and reading from it)* – 'a huge creature, luminous, ghostly, and spectral'. Mortimer has cross-examined them, all hard-headed countrymen, and all tell the same story of this dreadful apparition, exactly corresponding to the hell-hound of the legend. There is now a reign of terror in the district, Holmes, and it is a hardy man who will cross the moor by night.	10
HOLMES	And you, a trained man of science, believe it to be supernatural?	
WATSON	I do not know what to believe.	
HOLMES	Well, you must admit that the footprint was material.	

luminous *'giving out light'*

supernatural *'not belonging to the natural world'; to do with ghosts or magic.*

material *Something which could be seen or touched.*

WATSON   The original hound was material enough to tug a man's
throat out, and yet he was diabolical as well.   20

HOLMES   I see you have quite
gone over to the
supernaturalists,
Watson. I trust you
will permit me to
confine my
investigations to
the happenings of
this world. Pass me
that sketch again
will you? *(WATSON
hands him a sheet of
paper, which he
discusses.)* So Sir
Charles had walked
along this alley of
yew trees, which
leads from
Baskerville Hall. It's   30

about eight feet across and at one point there is a gap with   40
a gate in it, leading to the moor . . . Sir Charles's body was
found about fifty yards beyond that gap, assuming that he
had walked from the house . . . and the beast's prints were
seen between the body and the moor gate, which was
closed and padlocked.

WATSON   But only about four feet high, so anybody could have got
over it. Or anything.

HOLMES   *(Giving WATSON a brief withering look.)* And Sir Charles had
evidently been standing by the gate for five minutes or so.

---

diabolical *To do with the devil. (See the note on page 19.)*

WATSON	How do you know that?	50
HOLMES	We have Mortimer's evidence that the ash had fallen twice from Sir Charles's cigar.	
WATSON	Of course.	
HOLMES	And that change in the footprints between the gate and where the body was found. What do you make of that?	
WATSON	Mortimer reported that Sir Charles had walked on tiptoe down that portion of the alley.	
HOLMES	That was only his interpretation of the evidence. Why should a man have walked on tiptoe down his own path?	
WATSON	What then?	60
HOLMES	He was running, Watson – running desperately, running for his life, running until he burst his heart and fell dead upon his face.	
WATSON	Running from what?	
HOLMES	There lies our problem. There are indications that the man was crazed with fear before ever he began to run.	
WATSON	How can you say that?	
HOLMES	I am presuming that the cause of his fears came to him across the moor. Only a man who had lost his wits would have run from the house, instead of towards it.	70
WATSON	I see.	
HOLMES	Then again, whom was he waiting for that night, and why was he waiting for him in the Yew Alley, rather than in his own house?	
WATSON	You think he was waiting for someone?	
HOLMES	The man was elderly and infirm. Is it natural that he should stand for five or ten minutes, on a damp evening, near to the moor which terrified him, unless he was waiting for	

someone? *(With sudden impatience.)* Agh! If only I had been called at once. That gravel path, a page on which I might have read so much, has long since been smudged by the rain and defaced by the clogs of curious peasants. Oh, Dr Mortimer, Dr Mortimer, to think that you should not have called me in! You have indeed much to answer for.

The front door-bell rings.

And this will be our country practitioner, but this time not alone, I suspect. *(He walks to the door and opens it.)* Come in, gentlemen!

DR MORTIMER enters with the man we have seen in the hotel room.

HOLMES   *(Extending his hand to the stranger.)* Sir Henry Baskerville, if I am not mistaken.

SIR HENRY   How do you do, Mr Holmes, Dr Watson. My friend, Dr Mortimer has acquainted you with the distressing story of my uncle's death, I believe.

HOLMES   He has. My condolences. I am sorry that I did not have the opportunity to investigate the case when it arose. I observed some newspaper comment at the time, but was exceedingly preoccupied by that little affair of the Vatican cameos, and in my anxiety to oblige the Pope, I lost touch with several interesting English cases.

DR MORTIMER   But you will assist us now, Mr Holmes?

HOLMES   If I can. Please take a seat, gentlemen. Sir Henry, you are the late Sir Charles's only heir, are you not?

SIR HENRY   That's right. I'm his nephew. There were three brothers: Charles was the oldest, my father came next and then there

clogs *Heavy footware worn by the local country people.*

cameos *Small pieces of carved stone, no doubt extremely precious.*

	was a younger brother, Rodger. *(Laughs)* A bit of a black sheep, by all accounts, and the image of the wicked Sir Hugo. He made England too hot to hold him, fled to Panama, and died there in 1876 of yellow fever. I'm the last of the Baskervilles, Mr Holmes.
HOLMES	I see.
SIR HENRY	So what do you make of this hell– hound business?
HOLMES	*(Turning to MORTIMER.)* Dr Mortimer, put into plain words, the matter is this. In your opinion there is a diabolical agency which makes Dartmoor an unsafe abode for a Baskerville – Is that your opinion?
MORTIMER	At least I might go to the length of saying that there is some evidence that this may be so.
HOLMES	Exactly. But surely if your supernatural theory be correct, it could work as much evil on this young man in London as it could in Devonshire. A devil with merely local powers, like a parish council, would be too inconceivable a thing.
MORTIMER	You put the matter more flippantly, Mr Holmes, than you would probably do if you were brought into personal contact with these things.
HOLMES	Hmm. And I gather from your agitation this morning that there have been further developments?
	MORTIMER looks at SIR HENRY, who sighs and reluctantly takes the letter from his pocket.

110

120

130

a bit of a black sheep *The 'bad' member of the family.*

a diabolical agency *'some power of the devil'*

like a parish council *Holmes's mocking comparison of a 'local devil' with a parish council shows what he thinks of the idea that the hound might be supernatural.*

flippantly *'not taking it seriously'*

SIR HENRY	Dr Mortimer thought I should show you this. Some foolery sent to my hotel. Only a joke, as like as not.
	Watson takes the letter and reads out the address before handing it to HOLMES.
WATSON	'Sir Henry Baskerville, Northumberland Hotel'. Postmarked 'Charing Cross'; yesterday's date.
HOLMES	*(Without opening the letter.)* Who knew you were going to the Northumberland Hotel?
SIR HENRY	No one could have known. We only decided after I had met Dr Mortimer at the railway station.
MORTIMER	And I had been staying with a friend. There was no possible indication that we intended to go to that hotel.
HOLMES	Hmm. Someone seems to be very deeply interested in your movements.
	HOLMES takes out the sheet of paper.
SIR HENRY	You'll see it's all made up from printed words, cut up and pasted together.
HOLMES	Yes. Might I trouble you for yesterday's Times, Watson? *(He opens it and leafs through, rapidly running his finger up and down the columns.)* Ah! Capital article this on trade. Permit me to give you an extract from it. *(Reads.)* '. . . it stands to reason that such laws will in the long run reduce the value of our imports and keep away wealth from the country . . .' Admirable sentiments, Watson, don't you agree?
	All three look slightly puzzled.
WATSON	I don't know much about trade and that sort of thing, but it seems to me we've got a bit off the trail as far as that note is concerned, Holmes.
HOLMES	On the contrary, I think we are particularly hot upon the trail. See here *(showing them the article)*: 'reason', 'value', 'keep away', 'from the' – Don't you see now whence these

140

140

150

	words have been taken?
SIR HENRY	By thunder, you're right! So somebody cut out this message with scissors –
HOLMES	Nail–scissors. You can see that they were very short–bladed, since the cutter had to take two snips over 'keep away'.
SIR HENRY	– Nail scissors, and then stuck the words on with paste –
HOLMES	Gum.
SIR HENRY	Gum. Anything else you can tell, Mr Holmes?
HOLMES	The use of The Times newspaper tells us that we are dealing with an educated man. And you will observe that the lines 160 are very untidily pasted together. That may point to carelessness, or possibly to agitation and hurry on the part of the cutter. And yet there was no hurry: any letter posted yesterday would undoubtedly reach the hotel in time. Did the sender fear an interruption? And from whom? Sir Henry, has anything else of interest happened to you since you have been in London?
SIR HENRY	Why, no, Mr Holmes, I think not.
HOLMES	You have not observed anyone follow or watch you?
SIR HENRY	I seem to have walked right into the thick of a dime novel. 170 Why in thunder should anyone follow or watch me?
HOLMES	We are coming to that. You have nothing else to report to us before we go into this matter?
SIR HENRY	Well, it depends on what you think worth reporting.
HOLMES	I think anything out of the ordinary routine of life well worth reporting.

paste . . . Gum *Holmes likes to make sure that facts are recorded correctly, down to the finest detail.*

dime novel *A cheap American detective story.*

SIR HENRY	*(Smiling.)* Well, I'm a stranger to this country, but is it ordinary to have one of your boots stolen?
HOLMES	You have lost one of your boots?
MORTIMER	My dear sir, it is only mislaid. You will find it when you return to the hotel. What is the use of troubling Mr Holmes with trifles of this kind?
SIR HENRY	Well, he asked me for anything outside the ordinary routine.
HOLMES	Exactly. However foolish the incident may seem. You have lost one of your boots, you say?
SIR HENRY	Well, mislaid it anyhow. I put them outside my door last night and there was only one this morning. The worst of it is, I only bought them yesterday in the Strand and have never even worn them.
HOLMES	If you have never worn them, may I ask why you put them out to be cleaned?
SIR HENRY	They were tan boots and had never been varnished, so I put them out.
HOLMES	It seems a singularly useless thing to steal. I confess that I share Dr Mortimer's belief that it will not be long before the missing boot is found.
WATSON	But what about this letter?
MORTIMER	I find it worrying. It seems to show that someone knows more than we do about what goes on upon the moor.
HOLMES	Yes, but that the someone is not ill-disposed towards Sir

180

190

200

trifles *'small, unimportant matters'*

the Strand *A main street near Trafalgar Square in London.*

tan boots *Sir Henry's new boots were in a light-coloured leather and would stain easily. Varnishing would provide a protective covering.*

Henry, since they warn him of danger.

SIR HENRY Or it may be that they wish for their own purposes to scare me away.

HOLMES Well, of course, that is possible also. *(Standing.)* Dr Mortimer, I am very much indebted to you for introducing me to a problem which presents several interesting alternatives.

SIR HENRY Well, whatever they are, my answer is fixed. There is no devil in hell, Mr Holmes, and there is no man upon earth 210 who can prevent me from going to the home of my own people, and you may take that to be final! Now, it's half past eleven and I'm going back to my hotel. Suppose you and Dr Watson come round and lunch with us at two. I'll be able to tell you more then about how this thing strikes me.

HOLMES Thank you. Shall I have a cab called?

SIR HENRY I'd prefer to walk, for this affair has flurried me rather.

MORTIMER I'll join you in a walk with pleasure.

HOLMES Oh, one more question before you leave, Dr Mortimer. You 220 say that before Sir Charles Baskerville's death, several people saw this apparition on the moor?

MORTIMER Three people did.

HOLMES Did any see it after?

MORTIMER I have not heard of any.

HOLMES Thank you. Good morning.

---

cab At that time, people like Holmes travelled everywhere by horse-drawn hansom cab (usually just called 'a hansom'), a covered two-wheeled vehicle for two passengers, with the driver mounted behind and reins over the roof.

flurried 'disturbed'; 'upset'

HOLMES remains still until the door closes behind his guests. Then he leaps into action.

Your hat, Watson, quick! Not a moment to lose!

He rushes out. WATSON hurriedly finds his stick and runs after him.

230

Cross-fade to . . .

DISCUSSION: As a class, discuss what you think might be the reason behind the disappearance of one of Sir Henry's boots. How might it be connected to the mystery of Sir Charles's death?

WRITING AND DISCUSSION: Note down every piece of evidence you can find about the death of Sir Charles. Look at each item and discuss how important you think it might be. What clues do you think you now have in solving the mystery of his death?

WRITING: In scene 4, we find out that someone has sent Sir Henry a note. Create your own mysterious note by cutting words and phrases from a newspaper, and then write the scene in which Holmes finds out where it comes from and makes some deductions about the person who composed it.

ACT 1 ❖ SCENE 5

Baker Street. There is a sound of horses hooves and wheels upon cobble, street traders and the calls of passing pedestrians. HOLMES re-enters from another direction, closely followed by WATSON.

WATSON	Shall I run and stop them?	1

HOLMES	Not for the world, my dear Watson. I am perfectly satisfied with your company, if you will tolerate mine. Our friends are wise, for it is certainly a very fine morning for a walk. Ah! *(indicating with his stick)* There they are. Just look in this very interesting shop window for a moment, my good fellow, will you?

They look out into the audience, as though staring in a shop window, but HOLMES surreptitiously turns his head to look over his shoulder.   10

Yes, as I thought.

WATSON	Hmm?

HOLMES	Don't turn so obviously, Watson. There is our man, in that hansom. He's moving on. Now, let's follow. We'll have a good look at him if we can do no more.

They walk across the stage and stop again.

What can you see of him?

WATSON	A bushy black beard . . . Piercing eyes . . . He's seen us!

HOLMES	Quick, Watson!

*They rush off in pursuit, but as we hear the scrape of the cab's   20
wheels and the sound of galloping hooves receding into the
distance, HOLMES and WATSON come to a stop after a few*

steps, panting from their fruitless exercise.

HOLMES   (*Bitterly.*) There now! Was ever such bad luck and bad
          management too! Watson, Watson, if you are an honest
          man, you will record this also and set it against my
          successes. Why did I not hail a cab myself and go to the
          hotel to await our mysterious bearded friend? By our
          indiscreet eagerness we have betrayed ourselves and lost our
          man.   30

WATSON   Who was he?

HOLMES   I have not the slightest idea. I could only swear to the
          beard, from which I gather that, in all probability it was a
          false one.

WATSON   A spy?

HOLMES   Well, it was evident from what we had heard that
          Baskerville has been very closely shadowed since he has
          been in town. But we are dealing with a cleverer man that I
          had thought, Watson. He was a step ahead of us. So wily
          was he that he had not trusted himself on foot, but had   40
          availed himself of a cab, so that he could dash off at a
          moment's notice.

WATSON   What a pity we did not get the number of the cab!

HOLMES   My dear Watson, clumsy as I have been, you surely do not
          imagine that I neglected to get the number. 2704 is our
          man. Come in here.

They turn to one side.

ACT 1 ❖ *SCENE 6*

We hear a bell ring as they enter an office and the sounds of the street recede, to be replaced by the clatter of typewriters. HOLMES is greeted by a man wearing a waistcoat, black sleeve-protectors and an eye-shade.

POTTER	Why, it's Mr Holmes! How are you, sir?	1
HOLMES	Very well, thank you. This is my friend, Dr Watson.	
POTTER	It is a pleasure to meet you, Sir. Your friend once saved my good name, as you must of course know.	
HOLMES	This is Mr Potter, Watson, manager of the District Messenger Service, a splendid body of young fellows –	
POTTER	*(Quoting from their advertisement.)* "Prepared to go anywhere and do anything at duty's call by night or day!"	
HOLMES	*(Laughs.)* And I have some recollection, Potter, that you had among your boys a lad named Cartwright, who showed some ability during the investigation?	10
POTTER	Yes, sir, he is still with us. *(Calls out.)* Cartwright!	
HOLMES	This Cartwright is a bright young fellow, Watson, and just the man to visit every hotel in the neighbourhood of Charing Cross, search through the wastepaper and find the copy of The Times from which the words were cut. It will then be a matter of examining the register. The odds are enormously against his finding anything, but it is an	

District Messenger Service *As there were very few telephones at this time, people communicated by written messages, many carried across London by a team of boys, others further afield by telegram or 'wire' (see note on page 28).*

opportunity we cannot miss. Then it only remains for us to find out by wire the identity of cabman, number 2704.

2(

WATSON   Yes. From one source or another, we ought to have learned something by this evening.

HOLMES   (*Chuckling.*) Spectral hounds, anonymous letters and false beards: this case is proving to be more intriguing than I had thought. And I believe we are up against a worthy adversary.

Cross-fade to . . .

wire *Another name for a telegram – a message sent by telegraph, using electric current along wires.*

adversary *'opponent'; 'enemy'*

ACT 1 ❖ SCENE 7

*A London Street. Over the background traffic noises, we hear the sound of a hansom
cab coming to a standstill and, from off-stage, the voice of its passenger.*

PASSENGER (*Off-stage.*) Thank you, cabbie. You have done well.   1

CABMAN Oh! Thank you, sir!

*The passenger enters. He
is wearing a heavy cape,
with the hood drawn over
his head, but we can just
make out a square-cut,
bushy black beard. He is
about to stride off, but
stops, turns and calls
after the cabman.*   10

PASSENGER Oh, cabbie!

CABMAN (*Off-stage.*) Sir?

PASSENGER In case anyone should ask you, it
might interest you to know that you
have been driving Mr . . . (*pause for
effect*) . . . Sherlock Holmes! (*And he
roars with laughter as he strides off
at a swift pace.*)

Lights dim to black-out.   20

WRITING: Note down everything you think you know about Holmes's
'worthy adversary'. What kind of a person is he (or she)?

ACT 1 ❖ SCENE 8

The hotel room. SIR HENRY is in a bad temper again. WATSON is looking under cushions, HOLMES looking thoughtful, the MANAGER looking extremely nervous.

SIR HENRY	Seems to me you're playing me for a sucker in this hotel!
MANAGER	Sir, I promise you, this is the first time such a thing has ever happened.
SIR HENRY	The second time! The second! That is why I am so angry. Yesterday I lose a tan boot. Today it mysteriously returns. But what do I find? I have now lost a black boot!
HOLMES	A black boot?
SIR HENRY	Yes, sir, and I mean to find it! Last night they took one of my new tan boots, and this morning it's one of my old black ones. Either I get that boot back by sundown, or –
MANAGER	*(Backing out of the door.)* It will be returned, sir, I promise you, or the Northumberland Hotel will buy you some new boots.
SIR HENRY	*(Calling after him.)* I don't want a new pair. I want the other half of my old ones! *(To HOLMES.)* I'm sorry, Mr Holmes. You must excuse my getting angry over such a trifle.
HOLMES	I think it's well worth troubling about.
SIR HENRY	Why, you look very serious over it.
HOLMES	How do you explain it?

---

sundown *Having been brought up in Canada, Sir Henry talks of 'sundown' rather than 'sunset'.*

SIR HENRY	I just don't attempt to explain it. It seems the very maddest, queerest thing that ever happened to me.	20
HOLMES	(*Thoughtfully.*) The queerest perhaps. And one that makes me think that your decision to depart for Baskerville Hall is a sound one and should be acted upon without delay. There is a ten-thirty express from Paddington Station tomorrow morning. I would strongly advise you to take it. I have ample evidence that you are being dogged in London and, amid the millions of this great city it is difficult to discover who these people are or what their object can be. (*To Mortimer.*) Dr Mortimer, you did not know that you were both followed this morning from my house?	30
MORTIMER	(*Shocked.*) Followed! By whom?	
HOLMES	That, unfortunately, is what I cannot tell you. Have you among your neighbours or acquaintances on Dartmoor any man with a black, full beard?	
MORTIMER	No – or, let me see – Why, yes. Barrymore, Sir Charles's butler.	
HOLMES	Indeed! Where is Barrymore now?	
MORTIMER	He is in charge of the Hall.	
HOLMES	That can, of course, be checked. We will send a telegram, 'To Mr Barrymore, to be delivered into his own hand.' That should let us know before evening whether Barrymore is at his post in Devon, or not.	40
SIR HENRY	Who is this Barrymore, anyhow?	
MORTIMER	The son of the old caretaker, who is dead. He and his wife seem to be a very respectable couple. The family have looked after the Hall for four generations.	
HOLMES	Did Barrymore profit at all by Sir Charles's will?	
MORTIMER	He and his wife had five hundred pounds each.	
HOLMES	Really? Did they know they would receive this?	50

MORTIMER	Yes. Sir Charles was very fond of talking about the provisions of his will.
HOLMES	That is very interesting.
MORTIMER	I hope you do not look with a suspicious eye upon everyone who benefited. I myself received a thousand pounds.
SIR HENRY	And, if you're interested, Mr Holmes, the amount that comes to me is close on seven hundred and forty thousand.
WATSON	*(Surprised)* Dear me! That is a stake for which a man might well play a desperate game.
HOLMES	Or a woman, Watson.

60

Dim to black-out.

provisions of his will *The arrangements he had made for leaving money to people after his death. (See note on page 33.)*

ACT 1 ❖ SCENE 9

A kitchen. A woman is hurriedly putting together a basket of food. It could be for a picnic, were it not that her movements are agitated and her expression anxious. Now and then she goes to the door, in fear of being discovered at what is clearly a secret activity. Having wrapped up the last of the provisions, she picks up a bundle of clothes from the floor and, making a final check to see that the coast is clear, she takes a small lantern from the wall and, looking fearfully over her shoulder, silently makes her exit.

Dim to black-out.

the last of the provisions *Here the word means 'supplies of food and drink'.*

DISCUSSION: As a class, discuss who the mysterious woman is, who appears in scene 9. How might she fit in to the story?

STORYBOARDING: Sketch one frame to show what this scene might look like if it were part of a film, adding notes around the edges to explain what details of the set are visible, how the woman is dressed, and what she is doing.

ACT 1 ❖ SCENE 10

The tense silence is broken by a piercing train whistle and a blast of steam from off-stage to indicate that we are in Paddington Railway Station. The sounds of steam engines, slamming carriage doors and guards' whistles punctuate the whole scene. A porter enters, pushing some luggage on a trolley, and he is closely followed by HOLMES, WATSON, MORTIMER and SIR HENRY.

HOLMES	If I could accompany you myself, I would. But I fear that it is impossible for me at the present instant to be absent from London. One of the most revered names in England is being besmirched by a blackmailer, and only I can stop a disastrous scandal. But you will have a staunch companion in Dr Watson. There is no man who is better worth having at your side when you are in a tight place. No one can say so more confidently than I.	1
SIR HENRY	I am more grateful than I can say, Dr Watson. *(WATSON nods graciously.)* Dr Mortimer and I will see you on the train. We have a compartment reserved. Good bye, Mr Holmes and thank you.	10
HOLMES	Good bye, Sir Henry. Bear in mind one of the phrases in that queer old legend which Dr Mortimer has shown us, and avoid the moor in those hours of darkness when the	

revered *'respected'*

besmirched *Literally: 'made dirty'. A blackmailer is threatening to reveal information which will damage the good name of the family.*

compartment *Train carriages at that time were divided into separate sections which could be reserved in advance.*

queer *'strange, puzzling'*

powers of evil are exalted. *(Calls after him.)* And do not let Dr Watson leave your side!

A porter enters.

PORTER   One of you gentlemen Mr Holmes?

HOLMES   Yes?   20

PORTER   Two telegrams, sir. *(He hands them to HOLMES and leaves.)*

HOLMES   Ah, these should answer some of our questions. *(He tears them open and reads.)* 'Confirm telegram handed to Barrymore at the Hall – The Postmaster, Grimpen.' . . . 'Visited twenty-three hotels as directed, but sorry to report unable to trace cut sheet of Times – Cartwright.' There go two of my threads, Watson. There is nothing more stimulating than a case where everything goes against you. We must cast around for another scent.

WATSON   What about this Barrymore couple? Would it not be well in the first place to get rid of them?   30

HOLMES   By no means. You could not make a greater mistake. If they are innocent, it would be a cruel injustice, and if they are guilty, we should be giving up all chance of bringing it home to them. No, no, we will preserve them on our list of suspects along with Sir Henry's neighbours that Dr Mortimer has told me about. *(He takes a map from his pocket.)* This is the Ordnance map for our portion of the moor. I have marked the places which concern you. At the centre is Baskerville Hall. This small clump of buildings here is the hamlet of Grimpen where Dr Mortimer has his surgery. Within a radius of five miles there are, as you see, few scattered dwellings. Here is Lafter Hall, home of Mr   40

get rid of them *Watson is suggesting that the Barrymores should be dismissed from Sir Henry's employment; 'sacked'.*

Ordance map *A detailed map, these days called an Ordnance Survey map.*

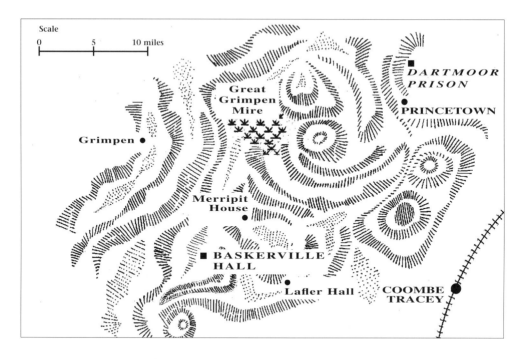

Frankland, by all accounts a rather bad-tempered
gentleman. This is Merripit House, the residence of a
naturalist called Stapleton, who lives with his sister, a
young lady of attractions. Then, fourteen miles away, the
great Dartmoor Prison at Princetown. Between and around
these scattered points extends the desolate, lifeless moor.
This is the stage upon which the tragedy has been played,
and upon which we may help to play it again.

50

WATSON   It must be a wild place.

HOLMES   Yes, the setting is a worthy one. If the devil did desire to
have a hand in the affairs of men –

a young lady of attractions *Holmes's rather roundabout way of referring
to an attractive young woman.*

WATSON	Then you are inclining to the supernatural explanation?
HOLMES	The devil's agents may be flesh and blood, may they not? There are two questions awaiting us at the outset. The one is whether any crime has been committed at all. The second is, if yes, what is the crime and how was it committed?
WATSON	I will do my best to find answers to them.
HOLMES	You have arms, I suppose?
WATSON	Yes, I thought well to take them.
HOLMES	Most certainly. Keep your revolver near you night and day and never relax your precautions.
WATSON	What did you learn from the cabman?
HOLMES	*(Roaring with laughter.)* Only that our bearded stranger announced himself as Mr Sherlock Holmes and was deposited at Waterloo Station! He had spotted me, knew I would trace the cabman, and so sent back this audacious message. Yes, Watson, this time we have got a foeman worthy of our steel. I've been checkmated in London. I can only wish you better luck in Devonshire. But I'm not easy in my mind about it.
WATSON	About what?

60

70

arms *Watson frequently carried a gun in some of his more dangerous adventures.*

never relax your precautions *Holmes is anxious that Watson should never become careless and ease up on safety measures.*

audacious *'bold, impudent, cheeky'*

a foeman worthy of our steel *An expression, taken from a poem by Sir Walter Scott, which comes from fencing (a 'steel' being a sword). Holmes feels that they have an opponent good enough to match them in skill and daring.*

checkmated *Now Holmes uses an expression from chess, meaning 'defeated'.*

HOLMES   About sending you. It's an ugly business, Watson, an ugly, dangerous business, and the more I see of it the less I like it.

WATSON   *(Laughing.)* You needn't worry about me, Holmes. *(He shakes HOLMES'S hand and strides off, shouting after him.)* I will write as soon as we reach Baskerville Hall. Good bye!

HOLMES   *(Seriously, to himself.)* Yes, my dear fellow, you may laugh.   80
                    But I give you my word that I shall be very glad to have you back safe and sound in Baker Street once more.

                    We hear doors slamming, a guard's whistle and the sound of the train pulling away. HOLMES remains where he is, gazing along the platform after the departing train. As the lights dim, he slowly raises an arm in farewell.

                    END OF ACT ONE

DISCUSSION: As a class, discuss the mystery of Sir Henry's second lost boot. Why should the first boot return and a second one go missing? In what way do you think the incident will turn out to be important?

WRITING: Write Holmes's diary for the day on which Watson and the others leave for Dartmoor. What are his fears, his theories about Sir Charles's death and the threat to Sir Henry, and his plans to solve the case?

The Hound of the Baskervilles
Act 2 ❖ Scene 11

The lights come up on Baskerville Hall. Centre stage stands a single figure in the dress of a butler, tall, serious and with a bushy black beard. He remains motionless in the silence for several seconds, looking off-stage in the direction from which we now hear the sounds of people approaching. SIR HENRY enters, followed by Watson.

BARRYMORE	Good afternoon, Sir Henry. My name is Barrymore. Welcome to Baskerville Hall, sir.	1
SIR HENRY	Good afternoon, Barrymore. I have heard a great deal about you from Dr Mortimer. You have been a loyal servant to this family and I hope will serve me too. *(BARRYMORE nods and signals to a servant to take the luggage that has been brought in. SIR HENRY walks around, gazing up at the walls and ceiling of the great hall.)* It's just as I imagined it. Is it not the very picture of an old family home? To think that this should be the same hall in which for five hundred years my people have lived! It strikes me solemn to think of it!	10
BARRYMORE	Would you wish dinner to be served at once, sir?	
SIR HENRY	Is it ready?	
BARRYMORE	In a very few minutes, sir. You will find hot water in your rooms. *(He hesitates: there is clearly something difficult that he has to say.)* My wife and I will be happy, Sir Henry, to stay with you until you have made fresh arrangements, but you will understand – *(He breaks off, clearly awkward.)*	
SIR HENRY	Are you saying that your wife and you wish to leave?	
BARRYMORE	Only when it is quite convenient to you, sir.	20
SIR HENRY	But your family have been here for generations, have they not? I should be sorry to begin my life here by breaking an	

old family connection.

BARRYMORE   *(Emotional.)* I feel that also, sir, and so does my wife. But to tell the truth, sir, we were both very much attached to Sir Charles, and his death gave us a shock and made these surroundings very painful to us.

SIR HENRY   But what do you intend to do?

BARRYMORE   We intend to establish ourselves in some business, sir. Sir Charles's generosity has given us the means to do so. And   **30** now, sir, perhaps I had best show you to your rooms.

BARRYMORE exits. SIR HENRY and WATSON exchange troubled looks and then follow him. No sooner have they left, however, than WATSON returns – he has forgotten a small item of luggage and has returned to collect it. He is busy checking that his favourite novel is in the side-pocket, when he hears a sound. It is a woman sobbing. He straightens up, listens, and quietly walks around the hall to try to ascertain the source of this mournful noise. Unable to do so, he collects his bag, listens for a few more seconds and then leaves, as the lights dim to black out.

ACT 2 ❖ SCENE 12

The moor next morning. It is sunny and we hear the sound of bird-song. WATSON enters, out of breath, and collapses on to a hillock. He looks up as a voice hails him from off-stage – 'DR WATSON!' – and is almost immediately followed by its owner, a man in his forties, wearing a straw hat and carrying a butterfly net. From his shoulder hangs a tin for specimens and he is panting from his exertions. It is SIR HENRY'S neighbour, MR STAPLETON.

STAPLETON	Dr Watson, you will, I am sure, excuse my presumption. Here on the moor we are homely folk and do not wait for formal introductions. You may possibly have heard my name from our mutual friend, Mortimer. I am Stapleton of Merripit House.	1
WATSON	*(Taking his offered hand.)* Your net and box would have told me as much, for I knew that Mr Stapleton was a naturalist. But how did you know me?	
STAPLETON	I have been calling on Mortimer, and he pointed you out from his surgery as you passed. I thought I would overtake you and introduce myself. I trust that Sir Henry is none the worse for his journey?	10
WATSON	He is very well, thank you.	
STAPLETON	We were all rather afraid that after the sad death of Sir Charles, the new baronet might refuse to live here. Sir Henry has, I suppose no superstitious fears in the matter?	
WATSON	I do not think that is likely.	
STAPLETON	Of course, you know the legend of the fiend dog which haunts the family?	
WATSON	I have heard it.	20

STAPLETON	It is extraordinary how credulous the peasants are around here! Any number of them are ready to swear that they have seen such a creature upon the moor! The story took a great hold upon the imagination of Sir Charles, and I have no doubt that it led to his tragic end.
WATSON	But how?
STAPLETON	His nerves were so worked up, that the appearance of any dog might have had fatal consequences upon his diseased heart.
WATSON	You think, then, that some dog did pursue Sir Charles, and that he died of fright in consequence?
STAPLETON	Have you any better explanation?
WATSON	I have not come to any conclusion.
STAPLETON	Has Mr Sherlock Holmes? *(He sees that WATSON is taken by surprise and laughs.)* It is useless for us all to pretend that we do not know you, Doctor Watson. The records of your detective friend have reached us even here. May I ask if he is going to honour us with a visit himself?
WATSON	*(Trying to give nothing away.)* He cannot leave town at present. He has other cases which engage his attention.
STAPLETON	What a pity! He might throw some light on that which is so dark to us. But you are perfectly right to be wary and discreet. *(He notices something far off.)* Ah, we are being observed.
WATSON	*(Following STAPLETON'S gaze to a distant hill.)* Who is it? And why is he armed?

30

40

---

credulous *They will believe anything.*

fatal consequences *The appearance of a hound could have caused Sir Charles's death.*

dark *'mysterious and unexplained'*

STAPLETON	It's a soldier. There's a convict escaped from the prison at Princetown. He's been out ten days now and the warders watch every road and every station, but they've had no sight of him yet.	50
WATSON	Do they normally send the army out for an escaped convict?	
STAPLETON	No, but this is no ordinary convict. This man would stick at nothing.	
WATSON	Who is he?	
STAPLETON	It is Selden, the Notting Hill murderer.	
WATSON	I remember reading about him.	
STAPLETON	Yes. He only avoided hanging because there were doubts about his sanity. *(Suddenly spotting a butterfly.)* Look! Cyclopides!	60

They turn to follow the insect's flight. Then Stapleton steps up on to the hillock and takes a deep breath.

It is a wonderful place, the moor. Undulating downs, like green Atlantic rollers, with crests of jagged granite, foaming up into fantastic surges. *(He laughs at his poeticism.)* You must forgive me, Dr Watson. But I never tire of the place. You cannot imagine the wonderful secrets it contains. It is so vast, and so barren, and so mysterious.

| **WATSON** | You know it well, then? |

Princetown *This is the location of Dartmoor Prison, still a place where dangerous and long-term prisoners might be sent.*

Notting Hill *An area in West London.*

Cyclopides *Conan Doyle has invented this name for a butterfly, based on the one-eyed giant in Homer's Odyssey.*

poeticism *In his enthusiasm for the moor, Stapleton's language has become rather poetic.*

STAPLETON I have only been here two years. Before that I was headmaster at a school in Yorkshire. But my hobby has led me to explore every inch of it. There are few men who know it better than I do.

WATSON Is it hard to know?

STAPLETON Very hard. Step up here. You see, for example, this great plain to the north, with the queer hills breaking out of it?

WATSON It would be a rare place for a gallop.

STAPLETON You would naturally think so, and the thought has cost people their lives before now. You notice those bright green spots scattered over it?

WATSON Yes, they seem more fertile than the rest.

STAPLETON *(Laughs.)* That is the Great Grimpen Mire. A false step yonder means death to man or beast. Only yesterday I saw one of the moor ponies wander into it. He never came out. I could see his head for quite a long time, craning out of the bog-hole, but it sucked him down at last. Even in dry seasons it is a danger to cross it, but after these autumn rains, it is an awful place. And yet I can find my way to the very heart of it and return unharmed.

Great Grimpen Mire *The name is made up, but there is a real Grimspound Bog on Dartmoor and also Fox Tor Mires. The Mire is boggy land in which people and animals can easily be sucked under and drowned.*

| WATSON | Then why should you wish to penetrate so horrible a place? | 90 |

| STAPLETON | It is where the rare plants and butterflies are. But I warn you never to go there; if you were to try, your blood would be on my head. |

Suddenly a long, low moan, indescribably sad, sweeps over the moor. From a dull murmur it swells into a deep roar and then sinks back into a melancholy, throbbing murmur once again.

STAPLETON looks at WATSON, with a strange expression.

Queer place, the moor!

| WATSON | But what on earth was it? |

| STAPLETON | The peasants say it is the Hound of the Baskervilles calling for its prey. I've heard it once or twice before, but never quite so loud. | 100 |

| WATSON | You are an educated man. You don't believe such nonsense as that. What do you think is the cause of so strange a sound? |

| STAPLETON | Bogs make queer noises sometimes. It's the mud settling, or the water rising, or something. |

| WATSON | No, no. That was a living voice. |

| STAPLETON | Well, perhaps it was. Did you ever hear a bittern booming? |

| WATSON | A what? | 110 |

| STAPLETON | A bittern – a very rare bird. Practically extinct in England now, but all things are possible on the moor. Yes, I should not be surprised to learn that what we have heard is the cry of the last of the bitterns. |

Your blood would be on my head *Stapleton is emphasising that he would feel responsible for Watson's death, were he to drown in the Mire.*

a bittern *A marsh bird, related to the heron, which made a strange booming sound. It was almost extinct at the time this story took place.*

WATSON	It's the weirdest, strangest thing I ever heard in my life.
STAPLETON	It's an uncanny place altogether. Look at the hillside yonder. What do you make of those?
WATSON	What are they? Sheep pens?
STAPLETON	No. They are what's left of the homes of the prehistoric people who inhabited the moor. Neolithic man. *(Spotting the butterfly.)* Ah! Cyclopides again! Excuse me, doctor, but it looks an excellent specimen!

He runs off and WATSON watches his progress, laughing quietly. He does not notice that a young woman, in fact, BERYL STAPLETON, has quickly and silently crept up to within a few yards of him and is startled when she speaks.

BERYL STAPLETON	*(In a penetrating whisper.)* Go back! Go straight back to London instantly!
WATSON	*(Amazed.)* Why should I go back?
BERYL STAPLETON	I cannot explain. But for God's sake do what I ask you. Go back and never set foot upon the moor again.
WATSON	But I have only just come.
BERYL STAPLETON	Man, man! Can you not tell when a warning is for your own good? Go back to London! Start tonight. Get away from this place at all costs! *(She looks off-stage anxiously, hearing STAPLETON'S return.)* Hush! My brother is coming! Not a word of what I have said.

STAPLETON returns and does not look altogether pleased to see his sister with WATSON.

STAPLETON	Hello, Beryl.

120

130

140

Neolithic man *Early stone-age humans. There are some important neolithic settlements on Dartmoor.*

BERYL STAPLETON	Well, Jack, you are very hot.
STAPLETON	Yes, I was chasing a cyclopides. *(Laughs ruefully.)* Without success, unfortunately. You have introduced yourselves I see.
BERYL STAPLETON	Yes, I was telling Sir Henry that it was rather late in the year to see the orchids on the moor.
WATSON	Oh, there has been a mistake. I am merely Sir Henry's friend. My name is Dr Watson.
BERYL STAPLETON	*(Extremely embarrassed.)* We have been talking at cross-purposes.
STAPLETON	*(A question in his eyes.)* Why, you had not very much time for talk.
BERYL STAPLETON	I spoke as if Dr Watson were a resident instead of a visitor. It cannot matter much to him whether it be early or late for orchids.
STAPLETON	No indeed. Dr Watson, our house is nearby. May we offer you lunch?
WATSON	Thank you.
BERYL STAPLETON	In that case, Jack, perhaps you should run on and warn cook to expect a guest.
STAPLETON	*(With some reluctance.)* Yes, you're probably right. Well, Dr Watson, we shall continue our talk in a few minutes. *(He bows, gives a meaningful look to his sister, and leaves them.)*
BERYL STAPLETON	*(Very flustered.)* I am sorry about the stupid mistake I made in thinking you were Sir Henry. Please forget the words I said, which have no application to you whatsoever.

150

160

with some reluctance *Stapleton clearly does not want Beryl to be alone with Watson.*

WATSON	But I can't forget them, Miss Stapleton. I am Sir Henry's friend, and his welfare is a very close concern of mine. Why were you so eager for him to return to London?
BERYL STAPLETON	A woman's whim, Dr Watson, nothing more.
WATSON	No, I remember the look in your eyes –
BERYL STAPLETON	You make too much of it, Dr Watson. I was shocked by the death of Sir Charles and am distressed that another member of the family should have come down here. I felt that he should be warned of the danger.
WATSON	But what is the danger?
BERYL STAPLETON	You know the story of the hound?
WATSON	I do not believe in such nonsense.
BERYL STAPLETON	But I do. If you have any influence with Sir Henry, take him away from a place that has always been fatal to his family.
WATSON	Let me ask you one more question, Miss Stapleton. Why did you not wish your brother to overhear what was said?
BERYL STAPLETON	*(Hesitant.)* My brother is very anxious to have the Hall inhabited. It gives work to the poor people on the moor. He would be angry if he thought I had tried to induce Sir Henry to leave. That is all. Now, we must go in for lunch. Please ask me no more questions.

170

180

She offers her arm and they walk off towards Merripit House. STAPLETON enters from another direction and watches them carefully and suspiciously. Suddenly he swings round, for he hears once again the long, unearthly baying of the phantom hound. The lights dim to black out, but not before registering an expression on his face of fear mingled with excitement.

190

The lights dim to black-out.

ACT 2 ❖ SCENE 13

The moor at night. An owl hoots and a figure creeps on stage, panting. In the moonlight we see – from the broad-arrow design on his pyjama-like outfit – that it is Selden, the escaped convict, and he is desperate for water. He throws himself to the ground and drinks from a bog noisily. Then, wiping his face, he gets up and fearfully scuttles off to conceal himself once more.

The lights dim to black-out.

 broad-arrow design *An arrow-head pattern printed on to convicts' clothing at that period.*

 DISCUSSION: As a class, discuss who the sobbing woman heard by Watson in scene 11 might be, and why she is distressed.

WRITING: Using the information provided by Stapleton in scene 12, produce a brief tourist brochure for this part of Dartmoor. Include his descriptions and any other information you have gathered from other parts of the play so far.

DISCUSSION: As a class, discuss the possible suspects so far (and consider exactly what crime they might have committed). Think about: Selden, the escaped convict; Barrymore, the butler, Stapleton, the naturalist; and Beryl Stapleton. Is there anyone else who ought to be on the list?

WRITING: Write Watson's first letter to Holmes in Baker Street, in which he informs Holmes about everything he has discovered so far, and lists the suspects.

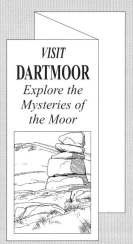

VISIT
DARTMOOR
Explore the Mysteries of the Moor

ACT 2 ❖ SCENE 14

Baskerville Hall, a few days later. SIR HENRY enters, followed by WATSON.

SIR HENRY	So Barrymore wasn't here when the telegram was sent?
WATSON	We can't be sure. All we know is what the Grimpen Postmaster told me. That he had sent a boy over here with the telegram and he had given it to Mrs Barrymore, who said that her husband was in the loft.
SIR HENRY	It doesn't look good, Watson. And then there's his wife, sobbing every night. What's distressing her? I tried to question Barrymore yesterday – I had passed on some of my unwanted clothes to him – but he denied that there was any problem.
WATSON	I'm afraid I have something even more worrying to tell you about Barrymore.
SIR HENRY	Go on.
WATSON	Last night, about two in the morning, I was aroused by a stealthy step passing my room. I rose, opened my door, and peeped out. A long shadow was trailing down the corridor, thrown by a man who walked softly down the passage with a candle in his hand. It was Barrymore, and there was something indescribably guilty and furtive in his whole appearance. I waited until he had turned into one of the rooms and then followed him and peeped round the corner

furtive *'stealthy and secretive'*

of the door. He was crouching at the window with the
candle still in his hand.

SIR HENRY   Which room was he in?

WATSON   It looks out westward. Of all the bedrooms, it has the best
view out on to the moor.

SIR HENRY   I knew that Barrymore walked about nights and I had a
mind to speak to him about it. Two or three times I have
heard his steps in the passage, coming and going, just about
the hour you name.   130

WATSON   Perhaps, then, he pays a visit every night to that particular
window.

SIR HENRY   Perhaps he does. If so, we should be able to shadow him,
and see what he is after. What do you say? Shall we sit up
tonight in my room and wait until he passes?

WATSON   Yes, and I think I shall come armed. Just in case.

The lights fade to black-out.

ACT 2 ❖ SCENE 15

The moor at night. Standing motionless on a hillock is a solitary figure, swathed in a cape. It is not SELDEN. Suddenly he hears a noise and disappears silently. Selden enters furtively and passes across the stage. (If technically possible, the solitary figure should be seen in silhouette behind the screen later to be used for back-projection.)

The lights fade to black-out.

STORYBOARDING: Sketch this scene in three or four frames, as though it were part of a film. Remember that the scene takes place at night and also think carefully about the appearance of the solitary figure. What should he look like, in your opinion? What different camera angles can you use to convey the mystery of the scene?

ACT 2 ❖ SCENE 16

Baskerville Hall. A downstairs clock strikes two, there is the unmistakable sound of a creaking stair, and the figure of BARRYMORE enters furtively, carrying a candle. He walks across the stage and then kneels at a window, pressing his face to the pane. As he lifts the light, SIR HENRY'S voice breaks the tense silence.

SIR HENRY	What are you doing here, Barrymore?	1
BARRYMORE	*(So agitated that he can hardly speak.)* Nothing, sir. It was the window, sir. I go round to see that they are fastened.	
SIR HENRY	On the second floor? This time of night? Look here, Barrymore, we have made up our minds to have the truth out of you, so it will save you the trouble to tell it sooner rather than later. No lies! What were you doing at that window?	
BARRYMORE	*(Anguished.)* Don't ask me, Sir Henry – don't ask me! I give you my word, sir, that it is not my secret, and that I cannot tell it. If it concerned no one but myself, I would not try to keep it from you.	10
WATSON	He must have been holding the candle as a signal. Let us see if there is any answer.	
	WATSON holds it up to the window for a few seconds and suddenly cries out.	
	There it is!	
BARRYMORE	No, no, sir, it is nothing – nothing at all. I assure you, sir –	
SIR HENRY	Move your light across the window, Watson. *(He does.)* See! The other moves as well! Now, you rascal, do you deny that it is a signal? Come, speak up! Who is your confederate out there, and what is this conspiracy that is going on?	20

BARRYMORE	*(More defiantly.)* It is my business, and not yours, and I will not tell.
SIR HENRY	Then you must leave my employment right away.
BARRYMORE	Very good, sir. If I must, I must.
SIR HENRY	And you go in disgrace. By thunder, you may well be ashamed of yourself. Your family has lived with mine for over a hundred years under this roof, and here I find you deep in some plot against me!

They have not noticed the silent entrance of MRS BARRYMORE.

MRS BARRYMORE	No, no, sir; not against you.
BARRYMORE	We have to go, Eliza. This is the end of it. You can pack our things.
MRS BARRYMORE	Oh, John, have I brought you to this? It is my doing, Sir Henry – all mine. He has done nothing except for my sake and because I asked him.
SIR HENRY	Speak out, then! What does it all mean?
MRS BARRYMORE	My unhappy brother is starving on the moor. We cannot let him perish at our very gates. The light is a signal to him that food is ready; and his light out yonder is to show the spot to which to bring it.
WATSON	Then your brother is –
MRS BARRYMORE	The escaped convict, sir. Selden, the criminal.

They are all silent for a moment.

BARRYMORE	That's the truth, sir. I said that it was not my secret. But now you will see that it was not a plot against you.

---

 confederate *'accomplice; a partner in crime'*

MRS BARRYMORE   He broke prison, sir, knowing that I was here and could not refuse to help him. Every day we have hoped that he is gone; but as long as he was there we could not desert him.   50

SIR HENRY   Is this true, Barrymore?

BARRYMORE   Yes, Sir Henry. Every word of it.

SIR HENRY   Well, I cannot blame you for standing by your own wife. Have you seen Selden recently?

BARRYMORE   No, sir. But the food is always gone when I return. Unless, of course, the other man has been taking it.

Both SIR HENRY and WATSON react to this.

WATSON   Another man?

BARRYMORE   Yes, sir.

WATSON   Have you seen him?   60

BARRYMORE   No, sir, but Selden told me about him a week ago. He's in hiding too, but he's not a convict as far as Selden can make out. Looks like a gentleman.

WATSON   Where's he living?

BARRYMORE   In the stone huts where the ancient folks used to live.

WATSON   But how about his food?

BARRYMORE   Selden says he's got a lad working for him and brings him all he needs, probably from Coombe Tracey. *(Becoming agitated.)* I don't like it, sir. There's foul play somewhere and there's black villainy brewing. I should be very glad to see   70 you on your way back to London again, sir. Look at Sir Charles's death. Look at the uncanny noises on the moor at

ancient folks *The neolithic people that Stapleton referred to. (See note on page 46).*

uncanny *'strange, worrying and inexplicable'*

	night. And that stranger hiding out yonder. What's he waiting for? What does it all mean?
SIR HENRY	What's to become of Selden?
BARRYMORE	Arrangements have been made, sir. In a few days he will be on his way to South America. For God's sake, sir, I beg you not to let the police know he is still alive on the moor. You can't tell on him without getting me and my wife into serious trouble. Please, Sir Henry.
SIR HENRY	What do you say, Watson?
WATSON	*(Shrugs.)* If he were safely out of the country it would relieve the tax-payer of a burden.
SIR HENRY	I guess we are aiding and abetting a felony, Watson. But, after what we have heard, I don't feel as if I could give the man up, so there's an end of it. All right, Barrymore. And there are some more old clothes of mine in the spare room. You had better let him have them.
BARRYMORE	God bless you, sir! It would have killed my poor wife had he been taken again. *(He and his wife turn to go, but he hesitates.)*
SIR HENRY	What is it?
BARRYMORE	You've been so kind to us, sir, that I should like to help you in return. I know something which I've never breathed to a mortal soul. It's about poor Sir Charles's death.
WATSON	*(Excited.)* Do you know how he died?

80

90

it would relieve the tax-payer of a burden *People would not have to pay out of their taxes to keep him in prison. Watson has a much more humane attitude here than when he earlier wanted Barrymore dismissed. (See note on page 35.)*

aiding and abetting a felony *Legal language for 'helping a crime to be committed'.*

BARRYMORE	No, sir.
WATSON	What then?
BARRYMORE	I know why he was at the gate at that hour. It was to meet a woman.
SIR HENRY	A woman!
BARRYMORE	Yes, sir.
SIR HENRY	And her name?
BARRYMORE	I don't know her name, sir, but I can give you her initials. Her initials are L. L.
SIR HENRY	How do you know this, Barrymore?
BARRYMORE	Sir Henry had a letter the morning he died. It was from Coombe Tracey and it was addressed in a woman's hand.
SIR HENRY	Well?
	BARRYMORE looks to his wife to take up the story.
MRS BARRYMORE	Only a few weeks ago, when I was cleaning Sir Charles's study, I found some burnt paper in the grate. It was the letter and only the end could be read. It said: 'Please, please, as you are a gentleman, burn this letter, and be at the gate by ten o'clock.' Beneath it were signed the initials L. L.
WATSON	Have you still got the paper?
MRS BARRYMORE	No, sir, it crumbled to ashes as I tried to move it.
WATSON	And you have no idea who 'L. L.' is?
BARRYMORE	No, sir. But there is a lady called Laura Lyons, the daughter of old Frankland across the moor. She runs a typewriting business in Coombe Tracey.
SIR HENRY	Could be the woman, Watson. *(To BARRYMORE.)* Why did you conceal this?
BARRYMORE	It came at the same time as Selden's escape, sir. We were

100

110

120

57

distracted. For another thing, we felt it was proper to tread carefully if there was a lady in the case.

SIR HENRY   You thought it might injure Sir Charles's reputation?

BARRYMORE   Exactly, sir.

SIR HENRY   Very good, Barrymore, you can go. *(THE BARRYMORES leave.)* What a night, Watson!   130

WATSON   Yes. A night of revelations. But are we any closer to unravelling this mystery? We strike Barrymore off our list of suspects, only to add this mysterious stranger on the moor.

SIR HENRY   And Laura Lyons too?

WATSON   Oh, yes. Anyone who asks to meet a man the very night he is found dead cannot be free of suspicion.

SIR HENRY   What will you do now?

WATSON   First write a letter to Holmes in Baker Street and report these latest developments.

SIR HENRY   And then?   140

WATSON   I suppose Holmes would visit Laura Lyons. *(Somewhat reluctantly.)* And then try to flush out this man on the moor, whoever he is.

SIR HENRY   Then, my dear Dr Watson, I guess that is precisely what you should do.

Cross-fade to . . .

a lady in the case *Barrymore wanted to avoid scandal if Sir Charles was involved with a woman.*

revelations *The facts revealed include the Barrymores' relationship with the escaped convict and the possible identity of the person who visited Sir Charles the night he died.*

DISCUSSION: As a class, discuss who the mysterious 'other man' on the moor might be. What is he doing there? How does he fit in to the story?

FREEZE-FRAME: In groups of three, create a freeze-frame, or tableau, for the moment when Sir Henry and Watson catch Barrymore at the window (page 53).

ARTWORK: Storyboard the opening of scene 16 in five or six frames, from the moment when Barrymore enters to Sir Henry's first speech.

IMPROVISATION: In pairs, improvise a scene in which Barrymore takes food and clothing to Selden, tells him what has happened and explains the arrangements for his escape to South America.

DISCUSSION: What were Watson's and Sir Henry's reasons for agreeing not to inform the police that Selden was still on the moor? As a class, discuss whether you think they were right. What do you think will happen as a result of their decision?

WRITING: Write Watson's next letter to Holmes. As before, up-date him on what you have discovered and say whom you suspect.

ACT 2 ❖ SCENE 17

LAURA LYONS'S office in Coombe Tracey. There is the sound of a single type-writer and the lights go up to reveal LAURA LYONS, seated at her desk, working. There is a knock on the door.

LAURA LYONS	Come in!
	She leaps up, smiling. But her smile fades as she sees it is a stranger.
WATSON	Mrs Lyons?
LAURA LYONS	Yes?
WATSON	My name is Dr Watson. I am staying on the moor, a neighbour of your father.
LAURA LYONS	*(Coldly.)* There is nothing in common between my father and me. I owe him nothing and his friends are not mine. If it were not for the late Sir Charles Baskerville and some other kind hearts, I might have starved for all that my father cared.
WATSON	It was about the late Sir Charles Baskerville that I have come here to see you.
LAURA LYONS	*(Reacting nervously, fingers playing over the type-writer keys.)* What can I tell you about him?
WATSON	You knew him well?
LAURA LYONS	I have already said that I owe a great deal to his kindness.
WATSON	Did you correspond with him?
LAURA LYONS	*(Angrily.)* What is the object of these questions?
WATSON	The object is to avoid a public scandal. It is better that I

should ask them than that the matter should pass outside my control.

LAURA LYONS (*Reluctantly.*) I certainly wrote to him once or twice to acknowledge his delicacy and generosity.

WATSON Did you meet him often?

LAURA LYONS Once or twice only, when he came to Coombe Tracey. He was a very retiring man and preferred to do good by stealth.

WATSON Then how did he know enough of your affairs to be able to help you? 30

LAURA LYONS Several gentlemen knew my situation and united to help me. One was Mr Stapleton, a neighbour and intimate friend of Sir Charles. It was through him that Sir Charles learned about my affairs.

WATSON Did you ever write to Sir Charles asking him to meet you?

LAURA LYONS (*Angrily.*) Really, sir, this is a very extraordinary question!

WATSON I am sorry, madam, but I must repeat it.

LAURA LYONS (*Hesitating momentarily.*) Then I answer – certainly not.

WATSON Not on the very day of Sir Charles's death?

LAURA LYONS (*Almost a whisper.*) No. 40

WATSON Surely your memory deceives you. I could even quote a passage of your letter. It ran 'Please, please, as you are a

---

delicacy *'sensitivity'*

retiring *He did not go out much.*

by stealth *'quietly and secretly'*

a very extraordinary question *In those days it was considered 'improper' for women to meet men in private. (See her question on page 62 about going 'at that hour to a bachelor's house'.)*

	gentleman, burn this letter and be at the gate by ten o'clock.'
LAURA LYONS	*(Almost fainting.)* Is there no such thing as a gentleman?
WATSON	You do Sir Charles an injustice. He did burn the letter, but some of it remained legible. You did write it?
LAURA LYONS	Yes. *(Defiantly.)* Why should I deny it? I have no reason to be ashamed of it. I wished him to help me. I believed that, if I had an interview, I could gain his assistance, so I asked him to meet me.
WATSON	But why at such an hour?
LAURA LYONS	Because I had just learned that he was going to London the next day.
WATSON	But why a rendezvous in a garden, rather than the house?
LAURA LYONS	Do you think a woman could go at that hour to a bachelor's house?
WATSON	Well, what happened when you got there?
LAURA LYONS	I never went.
WATSON	Mrs Lyons!
LAURA LYONS	No, I swear to you on all I hold sacred. I never went. Something intervened to prevent my going.
WATSON	What was that?
LAURA LYONS	That was a private matter. I cannot tell it.
WATSON	Mrs Lyons –
LAURA LYONS	All right. I will explain as far as I can. *(She stands and walks*

50

60

a gentleman A 'gentleman' would have protected the lady's honour and reputation by destroying the letter and keeping everything secret.

rendezvous 'an arranged meeting'

about agitatedly.) My life has been an incessant persecution from a husband whom I abhor. The law is on his side, but, at the time I wrote that letter, there was a chance that I could regain my freedom if certain expenses could be met. I   **70**
wrote to Sir Charles, hoping that he might help.

WATSON   But why did you not keep the engagement?

LAURA LYONS   Because at the last minute I received help from another source.

WATSON   *(He pauses, looking at her.)* I see. *(Standing.)* Thank you for your help, Mrs Lyons. It may be that I shall need to trouble you again.

He exits and she stands watching the door. Then she collapses into a chair, her head in her hands.

The lights dim to black-out.   **80**

incessant persecution *Her husband had constantly harassed her and treated her badly.*

abhor *'hate'*

The law is on his side *Married women had very few legal rights at that time. Divorce was extremely difficult and expensive.*

ACT 2 ❖ SCENE 18

The moor. There is a sound of birdsong and gusts of wind. The sun is about to set as WATSON enters, consulting his map and clearly looking for something.

WATSON Here we are. The neolithic settlements. 1

He looks around for a while and is about to leave when he hesitates and returns to a corner that he has not explored. With an exclamation of excitement, he snatches up a blanket, next to which are a few cooking utensils and other signs of occupation.

So this is where he lives. What's this? (*He reads from a sheet of paper.*) 'Dr Watson has gone to Coombe Tracey.' A child's writing? And why are they dogging me?

He peers off-stage, as though looking into the hut.

Only one way to get the answer: wait inside for the 10
occupant to return.

He crouches down and moves towards the exit, as though negotiating a low-arched opening. Then he turns to face the way he has come, sits down, takes out his revolver, checks the cartridges and places the gun on his lap to await his visitor. Several seconds have passed when WATSON suddenly sits bolt upright, for he has heard the snapping of a twig off-stage. He slowly lifts the revolver and points it in the direction of the sound of footsteps as they slowly approach his hiding-place. The footsteps stop, there is a moment's silence, and WATSON hears a 20 familiar, cold, ironical voice.

The neolithic settlements *The ruined dwellings of the stone-age people referred to by Stapleton. (See notes on pages 46 and 55.)*

dogging *'following, tracking'*

HOLMES	*(Off-stage.)* It is a lovely evening, my dear Watson. I really think you will be more comfortable outside than in.
	WATSON sits stupified for a second and then, with childish delight, leaps to his feet.
WATSON	Holmes! Holmes!
HOLMES	*(Entering.)* Come out. And please be careful with the revolver!
WATSON	*(Wringing him by the hand.)* I never was more glad to see anyone in my life.
HOLMES	Or more astonished, eh?
WATSON	Well, I must confess to it.
HOLMES	The surprise was not all on one side, I assure you. I had no idea that you had found my occasional retreat until I was within twenty paces of the door.
WATSON	My footprint, I presume?
HOLMES	No, Watson. If you seriously desire to deceive me, you must change your tobacconist. For when I see the stub of a cigarette marked Bradley, Oxford Street, I know that my friend Watson is in the neighbourhood. But how did you know anyone was here?
WATSON	Barrymore – and I will tell you more of him later – discovered that there was a man hiding on the moor, in addition to the escaped convict, that is.
HOLMES	Ah, yes, I have seen something of my criminal companion.
WATSON	But who has been bringing your supplies?

30

40

ironical *With a kind of 'dry' humour.*

Cartwright *Cartwright, one of the District Messenger boys, had helped Holmes on an earlier case, and was known to be reliable. (See page 27.)*

HOLMES	The admirable Cartwright, of course. Remember our visit to the District Messengers' Office? Mr Potter kindly leant me Cartwright's services for the duration. And I see he has left me a note. *(HOLMES reads it.)* So you have visited Mrs Laura Lyons, have you? Our researches have evidently been running on parallel lines.

50

WATSON	*(Rather hurt.)* But why did you not tell me you were here?
HOLMES	Had you known, you would no doubt have wished to communicate something to me, or in your kindness brought me some comfort or other. No, it was important that no-one should know of my presence here.
WATSON	*(Still upset.)* But –
HOLMES	*(Cutting him off.)* Now, to business. You are aware that a close intimacy exists between Mrs Lyons and this man Stapleton?

60

WATSON	I did not know of a close intimacy.
HOLMES	They meet and they write. Now, if I could use that fact to detach his wife –
WATSON	His wife?
HOLMES	Yes. The lady who passes for his sister is in reality his wife.
WATSON	But why the elaborate deception?
HOLMES	Because he saw that she could be much more use to him if she appeared to be unmarried.
WATSON	It is he then who is our enemy? It is he who dogged us in London?

70

HOLMES	So I read the riddle.

a close intimacy *Laura Lyons and Stapleton have a very close relationship.*

WATSON	And the warning letter sent to Sir Henry in London – it must have come from her!
HOLMES	Exactly.
WATSON	But are you sure of this, Holmes? How do you know the woman is his wife?
HOLMES	In the first of your extremely useful letters to me – brought, I should explain, via Baker Street, by Cartwright – you reported Stapleton's conversation with you. He told the truth when he said he had once run a school in Yorkshire, and from that detail it was easy to identify him from the register and ascertain that the woman was his wife.
WATSON	But then where does Mrs Laura Lyons fit in?
HOLMES	I am almost certain that Stapleton has offered to marry her after her divorce comes through.
WATSON	And when she finds out that he cannot?
HOLMES	Then, Watson, we will find the lady of service.
WATSON	But what is he after, Holmes? What is it all about?
HOLMES	Murder, Watson. Refined, cold-blooded, deliberate murder. But my nets are closing upon him and there is but one danger. And that is that *he* should strike before we are ready to do so. From now on you should not leave Sir Henry's side – Hark!
	A terrible scream – a prolonged yell of horror and anguish bursts out of the silence of the moor. They leap to their feet.
WATSON	Oh, my God!

80

90

of service *'useful to us'*

my nets Holmes often uses hunting images. Later he talks of the villain as *'fluttering in our net as helplessly as one of his own butterflies'* (See page 79).

HOLMES	*(Motionless, listening.)* Where did it come from, Watson?
WATSON	*(Pointing.)* There.

Again the agonised cry sweeps through the silence, but louder and nearer. Then they hear a new sound, a deep, menacing rumble.   100

HOLMES   The hound! Come, Watson! Great heavens, if we are too late!

As they rush off, the sound of the baying is heard once more, this time much nearer. A man rushes in, terrified and exhausted. It is difficult to identify him in the half light, but from his clothes it appears to be SIR HENRY. He stumbles, but, hearing the hound once more, staggers to his feet and runs off. He has not gone more that a few paces out of sight, however, before we   110 *hear a final, hideous cry of terror. HOLMES and WATSON rush in from a different direction. WATSON looks out of one exit, while HOLMES explores the other, leaving his friend alone on stage. WATSON is about to follow, when HOLMES enters, carrying the blood-stained and mutilated body in his arms.*

I was too late, Watson. We have failed. Sir Henry is dead.

WATSON buries his face in his hands as HOLMES carefully lays the body down on the ground.

WATSON   The brute! The brute! Oh, Holmes, I shall never forgive myself for having left him to his fate.   120

HOLMES   I am more to blame than you Watson. To ensure a water-tight case, I have thrown away the life of my client. It is the greatest blow which has befallen me in my career. But how could I know – how could I know – that he would risk his life alone upon the moor in the face of all my warnings?

WATSON   That we should have heard his screams and yet have been unable to save him!

HOLMES   Stapleton shall answer for this deed. But if we make one false move, the villain might escape us yet. Someone is coming! 130

A light from a swinging lantern precedes the entrance of two figures. As they aproach, we see that the first is BARRYMORE, and the second none other than SIR HENRY BASKERVILLE.

SIR HENRY   We heard the screams. *(Seeing the body.)* Who is the poor fellow? Why, Mr Holmes –

HOLMES and WATSON stand aghast. WATSON looks at SIR HENRY, then down at the body, then back to SIR HENRY.

WATSON   We thought –

Barrymore knows what has happened.

BARRYMORE   My God! *(He rushes to the body and examines it.)* It is as I 140
thought. *(Emotionally.)* This is Selden, Sir Henry. The escaped convict. He is wearing some of your old clothes, the ones you gave me.

SIR HENRY   *(Putting his hand on BARRYMORE'S shoulder.)* I am sorry, Barrymore.

BARRYMORE   I will need to inform my wife, sir.

SIR HENRY   Of course. I will help you carry him back to the Hall. Will I see you later, Mr Holmes?

HOLMES   Yes. We will follow you.

BARRYMORE and SIR HENRY carry the body off. 150

Do you recall the bizarre episodes of Sir Henry's lost boots, Watson?

WATSON   In the hotel? Yes, but –

---

  bizarre *'strange and inexplicable'*

HOLMES	Do you not see the explanation? The first stolen boot was returned and an older one taken in its place. Why? Because the new boot had not been worn and did not, therefore, carry Sir Henry's scent. The second one did, and it is that which has led the hound to his prey. The clothes have been the poor fellow's death
WATSON	My God!
HOLMES	*(Half to himself.)* But how did Selden know that the creature was on his trail?
WATSON	He heard him.
HOLMES	But hearing a hound upon the moor would not cause a hardened convict to risk giving himself away by screaming. And a greater mystery is why this hound should be loose tonight. *(Hearing footsteps.)* We have another visitor. Good lord!

It is STAPLETON, carrying a lantern and smoking a cigar. While pretending to express concern that someone might be in danger, he shows no surprise at coming face-to-face with HOLMES.

STAPLETON	I heard cries. I trust no one is harmed.
HOLMES	I am sorry to say there has been another death upon the moor.

16

17

18

STAPLETON	How terrible! Not Sir Henry?
HOLMES	Why Sir Henry in particular?
STAPLETON	Because I had suggested that he should come over this evening to dine with me and my sister. When I heard cries, 190 I was alarmed for his safety. This is awful. I feel so responsible.
HOLMES	Then it will be a reassurance to you to know that the dead man was not Sir Henry, but Selden the escaped convict.
STAPLETON	*(Scarcely able to disguise his amazement and disappointment, he drops his cigar.)* I am relieved beyond words. *(Trying to recover his composure.)* How did he die?
HOLMES	He appears to have broken his neck, falling down that ravine. Perhaps he was fleeing in the belief that he was about to be recaptured. His body has been taken back to the 200 Hall.
STAPLETON	Well, then my help is not required after all. *(He starts to go, but turns.)* By the way *(his eyes darting from HOLMES'S to Watson's.)* did you hear anything else besides his cries?
HOLMES	No. Did you?
STAPLETON	No.
HOLMES	Why do you ask?
STAPLETON	Oh, you know these stories the peasants tell about a phantom hound and so on.
HOLMES	We heard nothing of the kind. 210
	He nods, relieved. Then, with increased confidence, takes his leave.

good night Mr Sherlock Holmes. *Stapleton recognises Holmes' having seen him briefly from the hansom cab in Baker Street (See page 29).*

STAPLETON   Well, good night, Dr Watson. And . . . *(picking up his cigar)* good night Mr Sherlock Holmes. We have all been awaiting your arrival with eager anticipation.

He exits, more jauntily than a few minutes before.

WATSON   What a nerve the fellow has! I am sorry that he has seen you.

HOLMES   There was no getting out of it.

WATSON   What effect will it have upon his plans, now that he knows   22 you are here?

HOLMES   It will almost certainly drive him to desperate measures at once. He has failed tonight and will be impelled to try again as soon as he can.

WATSON   What do you propose doing next?

HOLMES   Three things, Watson and without delay. In the morning I will visit Mrs Laura Lyons, inform her that Stapleton is married, and get whatever evidence I can which will help to convict him. There is no doubt that Stapleton instructed her to write that letter asking Sir Charles to meet her at the   23 gate on that fateful night, but we must have her sworn confirmation that it is so. Secondly, you will send a wire to Inspector Lestrade at Scotland Yard, telling him that we will meet him off the ten-thirty from Paddington. Thirdly – *(He pauses, struggling for a second.)* yes, there is no other way – thirdly we will instruct Sir Henry to rearrange tonight's broken dinner engagement with the Stapletons for tomorrow evening.

WATSON   Are you sure, Holmes?

Inspector Lestrade *Lestrade has known Holmes for some time and often appears at the end of the adventures. Holmes needs a trustworthy policeman from Scotland Yard to arrest the villain when it is all over.*

| HOLMES | Yes. Sir Henry will be safe if he goes over to Merripit House in daylight. But, if my plan is to work, Stapleton has to believe that you and I have returned to London. And that means that Sir Henry has to believe it also, if he is to play his part convincingly. You and Lestrade can meet me at my hiding-place on the moor at sunset. We will make our move from there. The net must close in tomorrow night. | 240 |

Cross-fade to . . .

ARTWORK: Draw four frames of the storyboard of the opening of scene 18, where Watson enters one of the neolithic huts.

FREEZE-FRAME: In groups of five, create a freeze-frame for the moment on page 00 where Holmes and Watson, having retrieved the body, are interrupted by Sir Henry and Barrymore. (Remember that Holmes and Watson thought the body was Sir Henry!)

WRITING: Re-read the part of scene 18 where Stapleton arrives (from 'I heard cries . . .') to his exit. In pairs, note down what you guess Stapleton is thinking before each of his speeches and as he leaves. Compare your notes with other pairs'.

WRITING: Write down Laura Lyons's thoughts after Watson has left her. Remember to take account of what you learned on pages 66 and 67.

DISCUSSION: As a class, discuss what you think will happen when Holmes visits Laura Lyons and tells her that Stapleton is married.

DISCUSSION: As a class, discuss why you think Stapelton should be trying to kill Sir Henry. What does he hope to gain, and how, in your opinion?

DISCUSSION: As a class, discuss whether you think it is totally fair of Holmes to lie to Sir Henry about returning to London, and not inform him that Stapleton is planning to murder him.

ACT 2 ❖ SCENE 19

Baskerville Hall, an hour later. Enter SIR HENRY, with a glass in his hand, and BARRYMORE.

SIR HENRY	That will be all for this evening, Barrymore. You will need to comfort your wife.
BARRYMORE	Yes, sir. Whatever else, he was her only brother.
SIR HENRY	Of course. Good night.
BARRYMORE	Good night, sir.
	BARRYMORE exits as HOLMES and WATSON enter.
SIR HENRY	Ah, come in, Mr Holmes. I must say, it's good to be back here after that terrible business. Welcome to Baskerville Hall. This is the gallery, as you see. And here are my ancestors *(indicating portraits on the walls)*. Now, what do we do next? I'm in your hands, Mr Holmes. Whatever you tell me to do, I'll do.
HOLMES	*(Examining the portraits – in other words, gazing into the audience – as he speaks.)* Very good; and I will ask you to do it blindly, without always asking the reason.
SIR HENRY	Just as you like.
HOLMES	Then, to begin with – I believe your invitation to dine with Stapleton and his sister at Merripit House has been rearranged for tomorrow evening?
SIR HENRY	Yes. I hope that you will come also. They are very hospitable people, and I'm sure they would be very glad to see you.
HOLMES	I fear that Watson and I must go to London.

SIR HENRY	To London?
HOLMES	Yes. I think we should be more useful there at the present juncture.
SIR HENRY	*(His face expresses his disappointment and concern.)* I had hoped that you were going to see me through this business. The Hall and the Moor are not very pleasant places when one is alone.
HOLMES	My dear fellow, you must trust me implicitly and – as I said – do exactly what I tell you. You can tell your friends that we should have been happy to have come with you, but that urgent business required us to be in town. We hope very soon to return to Devonshire. Will you remember to give them that message?
SIR HENRY	If you insist upon it.
HOLMES	There is no alternative, I assure you.
SIR HENRY	*(Upset and offended by his friends' apparent desertion.)* When do you desire to go?
HOLMES	Immediately after breakfast. Watson will send a note to Stapleton to tell him that we regret that we cannot come.
SIR HENRY	I have a good mind to go to London with you. Why should I stay here alone?
HOLMES	Because it is your post of duty. Because you gave me your word that you would do as you were told, and I tell you to stay.
SIR HENRY	*(With obvious reluctance.)* All right, then, I'll stay.
HOLMES	One more direction! I wish you to drive to Merripit House.

30

40

juncture *'point of time'*

implicitly *'absolutely'; 'without questioning'*

	Send back your trap, however, and let them know that you intend to walk home.	5
SIR HENRY	*(Amazed.)* To walk across the moor?	
HOLMES	Yes.	
SIR HENRY	But that is the very thing which you have so often cautioned me not to do.	
HOLMES	This time you may do it with safety. If I had not every confidence in your nerve and courage, I would not suggest it, but it is essential that you should do it.	
SIR HENRY	Then I will do it.	
HOLMES	And as you value your life, do not go across the moor in any direction save along the straight path which leads from Merripit House to the Grimpen Road, and is your natural way home.	6
SIR HENRY	I will do just what you say.	
HOLMES	Thank you. If you follow those instructions to the letter, I think the chances are that our little problem will soon be solved. I have no doubt –	
	He breaks off, staring at one of the portraits.	
SIR HENRY	What is it?	
HOLMES	*(His eyes shining with amusement.)* Excuse the admiration of a connoisseur. Watson won't allow that I know anything about art, but these are a very fine set of portraits.	7
SIR HENRY	Well, I'm glad to hear you say so.	
HOLMES	I know what's good when I see it. That's a Kneller, I'll swear,	

to the letter *'in every detail'*

connoisseur *(pronounced conner-Sir) Somebody who enjoys something and knows a lot about it (in this case, art).*

that lady in the blue silk; and the stout gentleman with the wig ought to be a Reynolds. They are all family portraits, I presume?

SIR HENRY   Every one.

HOLMES   Do you know the names?

SIR HENRY   Barrymore has been coaching me in them, and I think I can 80
say my lessons fairly well.

HOLMES   Who is the gentleman with the telescope?

SIR HENRY   That's Rear-Admiral Baskerville. He served under Rodney in the West Indies.

HOLMES   And this Cavalier opposite me – the one with the black velvet and lace?

SIR HENRY   Ah, you have a right to know about him. That is the cause of all the mischief, the wicked Hugo, who started the Hound of the Baskervilles. We're not likely to forget him.

HOLMES   Dear me! He seems such a quiet, meek-mannered man, but I 90
daresay there was a lurking devil in his eyes.

SIR HENRY   *(Puzzled by HOLMES'S enthusiasm, given the seriousness of the evening's events.)* I dare say. Well, if you'll excuse me, gentlemen, I'll turn in. It's been a strange day.

HOLMES   Of course. Goodnight, Sir Henry.

SIR HENRY   Goodnight, gentlemen.

He goes. HOLMES, still looking at the portrait (that is, straight out into the audience), chuckles.

Kneller . . . Reynolds *Sir Godfrey Kneller and Sir Joshua Reynolds were famous portrait painters.*

Rodney *An 18th Century British admiral.*

Cavalier *Someone who supported the King in the English Civil War.*

HOLMES	Do you see anything there?
WATSON	What do you mean?

100

HOLMES	Is it like anyone you know?
WATSON	*(Squints and tilts his head to one side.)* There's a suggestion of Sir Henry about the jaw.
HOLMES	Just a suggestion perhaps. But wait an instant.

HOLMES stands on a chair and, holding up a light in his left hand, curves his right around the face, to cover the beard, ringlets and hat.

WATSON	*(Amazed.)* Good heavens! It's Stapleton! It could be his portrait.
HOLMES	Yes. Stapleton is an interesting example of a throw-back which appears to be both physical and spiritual. The fellow is a Baskerville – there can be no doubt.

110

WATSON	With designs upon the succession.
HOLMES	Exactly. If my surmises have been correct, Lestrade will bring with him evidence of Stapleton's position in the Baskerville family. Sir Henry's uncle, the black sheep, Sir Rodger, is supposed to have died childless in Panama. My guess is that he did not, and that Stapleton is his son. Come, Watson, let us retire. We have a full day ahead of us tomorrow. *(He strides off, then turns exultantly.)* We have him, Watson, we have him. And I dare swear that by

120

throw-back *An example of someone who shows characteristics or features of an ancestor. In this case, Stapleton both looks like the wicked Sir Hugo and is like him in character.*

surmises *'suspicions'*

My guess is that he did not *As in most things, Holmes is later proved right!*

retire *'go to bed'*

tomorrow night he will be fluttering in our net as helplessly as one of his own butterflies. A pin, a cork, and a card, and we add him to the Baker Street collection!

He exits, laughing. WATSON looks up at the portrait once more, shudders, and follows HOLMES out.

Lights fade to black-out.

 A pin, a cork, and a card *Items used by butterfly collectors to mount their specimens.*

ACT 2 ❖ SCENE 20

The moor, sunset the next day. A light fog begins to swirl about the moor. WATSON and INSPECTOR LESTRADE (a wiry bulldog of a man) enter from one direction, HOLMES from another.

HOLMES	*(Shaking Lestrade's hand.)* I am glad that you were able to join us, Lestrade. At least we shall take the London fog out of your throat and give you a breath of the pure night air of Dartmoor.
LESTRADE	Pleased to be of assistance, Mr Holmes. This looks like the biggest thing in years. Where is he?
HOLMES	Still in the house with Sir Henry. Oddly there is no sign of his wife. They have dined and, only five minutes ago, our friend Stapleton left his guest and appeared in the courtyard. I watched him go towards the out-buildings and heard a key turn in a padlock.
WATSON	The hound?
HOLMES	Almost certainly. From the evidence, he must usually keep the beast hidden in one of the disused tin-mines on the moor, bringing it here when he plans to let it loose. Did you find the information I asked for, Lestrade?
LESTRADE	Yes. You were right. Sir Rodger Baskerville did have a son: this is the man.

1

10

London fog *This is ironic: Holmes's plans are about to be endangered by Devon fog!*

tin-mines *People have mined for tin on Dartmoor for thousands of years and some of the ancient mines are still there.*

HOLMES	And a very dangerous one, of the old Sir Hugo strain. Are you armed?	20
LESTRADE	*(Smiling.)* As long as I have my trousers, I have a hip-pocket, and as long as I have a hip-pocket, I have something in it!	
HOLMES	Good! My friend and I are also ready for emergencies.	
LESTRADE	You're mighty close about this affair, Mr Holmes. What's the game now?	
HOLMES	A waiting game.	
LESTRADE	We are to wait here?	
HOLMES	Yes, this is where we shall make our ambush. But I begin to be uneasy . . . This fog. I fear it's moving towards us, Watson.	30
WATSON	Is that serious?	
HOLMES	Very serious indeed. The one thing on earth which could disarrange my plans. If Sir Henry isn't out in a quarter of an hour, the path will be covered. In half an hour we won't be able to see our hands in front of us.	

Several seconds pass. LESTRADE checks his revolver, WATSON paces a little, HOLMES stands motionless, gazing into the thickening fog. Suddenly HOLMES lifts a finger.

Thank God. I think I hear him coming. Yes *(looking out)*, there he goes. 40

A look of alarm comes to his face.

Listen!

There is a crisp, thin continuous patter from somewhere behind

---

As long as I have my trousers . . . *This is Lestrade's long-winded way of saying that he always carries a gun!*

close *'secretive'; 'not giving much away'*

them. By this time, the fog is thick, the light dim, and it is
difficult to make much out, but the men move outward and train
their revolvers in the same direction – (towards a screen, designed
to take back-projection, set in place during the fog and dim
light).

What happens next
should be sudden
and frightening.
Accompanied by
terrifyingly loud
sounds of snarling
and howling, an
image of an
enormous hound
flashes blindingly
on to the screen.
WATSON shouts
'My God, no!',
Lestrade throws
himself to the
ground, the hound's
dreadful noises grow
to an almost
unbearable volume,

50

60

and the men fire indiscriminately at the constantly fast-changing
images of fangs, fiery eyes and glowing muzzle before them.

HOLMES rushes off, shouting 'SIR HENRY!', there is a final shot
from off-stage and then a silence, broken only by the sound of
WATSON'S and LESTRADE'S panting. The lights come up just
enough to reveal the re-entrance of HOLMES, bearing a lantern
and supporting SIR HENRY. WATSON and LESTRADE scramble

70

indiscriminately *Without choosing carefully – in this case, without aiming
at a particular part of the target.*

	to their feet and the INSPECTOR thrusts a brandy flask between SIR HENRY'S teeth.
SIR HENRY	*(Barely whispering.)* My God! What was it? What, in Heaven's name, was it?
HOLMES	It's dead, whatever it was. We have laid the family ghost once and for ever. It was a blood-hound, or mastiff, but of huge size. You will find your man at the house, Lestrade.
WATSON	*(To LESTRADE.)* I will come with you.
HOLMES	But be careful. He will be armed.
	WATSON and LESTRADE exeunt.
SIR HENRY	But the flames?
HOLMES	Phosphorous. Or a cunning preparation of it. There was no smell to interfere with its power of scent. I owe you a deep apology, Sir Henry, for exposing you to this terror. I was prepared for a hound, but not such a creature as this. And the fog gave us little time to receive him.
SIR HENRY	You have saved my life.
HOLMES	Having first endangered it.
	WATSON and LESTRADE return, supporting STAPLETON'S wife. By her appearance, she has clearly been badly treated and seems only half-conscious. WATSON carefully sits her on the ground and wipes the sweat and tears from her face.
WATSON	The brute had imprisoned her in an upstairs room, bound and gagged, so that she could not warn Sir Henry.
SIR HENRY	But why did he want to kill me? I still don't –

80

90

Phosphorous *A chemical substance that glows in the dark.*

LESTRADE	Stapleton is not his real name. He is a Baskerville – your cousin: the only son of Sir Rodger.	100
SIR HENRY	*(Trying to take in this information.)* But I thought –	
LESTRADE	It appears he has lived most of his life in Central America. In Panama, where his father died. And to where he would no doubt have returned after your death, to claim his inheritance by letter. It was a devilish plan. *(Helping Sir Henry to his feet.)* Come, Sir Henry. Let me take you home, sir.	
SIR HENRY	*(Still suffering from the effects of the horrific attack, and bewildered by what he has been told.)* Home . . . Yes . . .	110
	Helped by LESTRADE, SIR HENRY slowly sets off for Baskerville Hall.	
BERYL STAPLETON	*(Opening her eyes and looking at WATSON.)* Is he safe? Has he escaped?	
WATSON	He cannot escape us, madam.	
BERYL STAPLETON	No, I did not mean my husband – Sir Henry? Is he safe?	
WATSON	Yes: quite safe.	
BERYL STAPLETON	Thank heaven! And the hound?	
WATSON	It is dead.	
BERYL STAPLETON	*(She gives a long sigh of relief.)* Thank God! Thank God! Oh, this villain! See how he has treated me! *(She pulls back her sleeves to reveal the mottled bruises and marks on her arms.)* But this is nothing – nothing! It is my mind and soul that he has tortured and defiled. I could endure it all – ill-usage, solitude, a life of deception, everything – as long as I could	120

---

defiled *'made dirty, polluted'*

his dupe and his tool *Someone he had deceived and used in his plot.*

atone *'make up for having done something wrong'*

still cling to the hope that I had his love . . . But now I know that in this also I have been his dupe and his tool.

HOLMES   You have no reason to shelter him any more, madam. Tell us, then, where we shall find him. If you have ever aided him in his evil, help us now and so atone.   130

She looks up and, aided by WATSON, manages to stand and then slowly walk away from the men. WATSON makes a move towards her, but is stopped by a gesture from HOLMES, who is watching her intently. She stops, some way from them, and gazes out over the moor.

BERYL STAPLETON   There is but one place where he can have fled. There is an old tin mine on an island in the heart of the Mire. It was there that he kept his hound and there also he had made preparations so that he might have a refuge. That is where he would fly.   140

HOLMES walks up to join her and holds his lantern out in the direction of her gaze.

HOLMES   No one could find his way through this fog into the Grimpen Mire tonight.

BERYL STAPLETON   *(Uttering a frightening laugh.)* He may find his way in, but never out. We planted sticks as markers, guiding wands to mark a pathway through the Mire from one dry island to the next. But he will never see them in the darkness and the fog.

WATSON has approached and joins HOLMES and 15
STAPLETON'S wife, looking out across the Mire. Suddenly
WATSON spots something in the bog.

WATSON   *(Pointing to the ground a few feet from them.)* Holmes! What's
that? Stuck in the mud?

He is about to dart forward, but HOLMES stops him.

HOLMES   Wait! This is the very edge of the Mire. One false step and
you could be lost in seconds. Here: grip my arm and don't
let go!

Held firmly by WATSON, HOLMES stretches forward along the
ground and reaches out to retrieve the object stuck in the mud. It 16
is an old black boot. HOLMES looks inside and reads the maker's
name.

'Myers, Toronto'!

WATSON   It is our friend Sir Henry's missing boot!

HOLMES   And worth a mud bath. Thrown here, no doubt, by
Stapleton in his flight.

WATSON   He must have kept it in his hand after using it to set the
hound on Sir Henry's track. He fled when he knew the
game was up, still clutching it, and hurled it away at this
point in his flight.   1?

HOLMES   *(Nods.)* We know at least that he came this far in safety.

STAPLETON'S WIFE looks at HOLMES and he recognises the
terrible mixture of emotions she must be experiencing. He takes
her arm and gently leads her off in the direction taken by SIR
HENRY and LESTRADE. WATSON stands alone on the edge of
the Great Grimpen Mire, as the lights dim until he is left in a
single spot. He looks up and addresses the audience.

WATSON   But more than that we were never destined to know,
though there was much which we might surmise. When we
returned the next day, there was no chance of finding   18

footsteps in the Mire, for the rising mud would have oozed swiftly in upon them. As we at last reached firmer ground beyond the morass we all looked eagerly for them. But no slightest sign of them ever met our eyes. *(Faint solo violin music begins.)* If the earth told a true story, then Stapleton never reached that island of refuge towards which he struggled through the fog upon that last night. Somewhere in the heart of the Great Grimpen Mire, down in the foul slime of the huge morass which had sucked him in, this cold and cruel-hearted man is for ever buried.

190

The light on WATSON dims to blackness and we are left with the sound of the violin.

The End

surmise *'work out, guess'* (Here it is a verb; on page 78 it is a noun.)

morass *'marsh, bog'*

HOT-SEATING: Hot-seat Holmes. Ask him, among other things, why he did not let Sir Henry know about his plan, and whether he was totally happy with the way things went.

ARTWORK: Draw four frames of a storyboard for the scene in which the hound appears (from 'Listen!' to the end of the stage directions).

ARTWORK: Draw up the family tree, to show exactly how Sir Henry and Stapleton are related. It will help to re-read Sir Henry's explanation on page 10.

HOT-SEATING: In groups of four, hot-seat Beryl Stapleton. Among other things, ask her how she feels about Stapleton and why she did not reveal earlier what was going on.

INTERVIEWING: In groups of five, one person is a journalist from a national newspaper, interviewing Holmes, Watson, Sir Henry and Beryl Stapleton. Each one should be asked about his or her view of events, including what they think has happened to Stapleton.

LOOKING BACK AT THE PLAY

1 DISCUSSION: CASTING THE ROLES

In pairs, discuss which film or television actors you would cst in each of the roles, noting down brief reasons to support your choices. Compare your ideas in a class discussion.

2 ARTWORK AND WRITING: DESIGNING A POSTER

Work in pairs on a poster to advertise a stage, television or film version of The Hound of the Baskervilles. First, discuss as a class the words and images that usually appear on a poster of this kind.

3 ARTWORK AND WRITING: A THEATRE PROGRAMME

Create a programme for a production of the play in the theatre. Remember to include the cast that you have decided on, as well as any maps or illustrations that would be helpful to the audience.

4 WRITING: A NEWSPAPER ARTICLE

Write a newspaper article for a national newspaper the day after the hound is killed. Include quotes from several characters and speculate on what might have happened to Stapleton.

5 NOTE-MAKING AND DISCUSSION: SHERLOCK HOLMES

In pairs, look back through the play and make as many notes as you can about Holmes's character and his abilities as a detective. Then discuss as a class why you think he has become the most famous detective in fiction.

6 DISCUSSION: ADAPTING FROM NOVEL TO PLAY

In pairs, read the extract from the novel on page 89. Discuss what the author has done in adapting the scene for the stage. (It can be found on pages 14 and 15.) How much of the original dialogue has been used, for example? What has been added and why? What are the strengths of the two different versions?

We heard the steps of our visitors descend the stair and the bang of the front door. In an instant Holmes had changed from the languid dreamer to the man of action.

'Your hat and boots, Watson, quick! Not a moment to lose!' He rushed into his room in his dressing-gown, and was back again in a few seconds in a frock-coat. We hurried together down the stairs and into the street. Dr Mortimer and Baskerville were still visible about two hundred yards ahead of us in the direction of Oxford Street.

'Shall I run on and stop them?'

'Not for the world, my dear Watson. I am perfectly satisfied with your company, if you will tolerate mine. Our friends are wise, for it is certainly a very fine morning for a walk.'

He quickened his pace until we had decreased the distance which divided us by about half. Then, still keeping a hundred yards behind, we followed into Oxford Street and so down Regent Street. Once our friends stopped and stared into a shop window, upon which Holmes did the same. An instant afterwards he gave a little cry of satisfaction, and, following the direction of his eager eyes, I saw that a hansom cab with a man inside which had halted on the other side of the street was now walking slowly onwards again.

'There's our man, Watson! Come along! We'll have a good look at him, if we can do no more.'

At that instant I was aware of a bushy black beard and a pair of piercing eyes turned upon us through the side window of the cab. Instantly the trap-door at the top flew up, something was screamed to the driver, and the cab flew madly off down Regent Street. Holmes looked eagerly round for another, but no empty one was in sight. Then he dashed in wild pursuit amid the stream of the traffic, but the start was too great, and already the cab was out of sight.

'There now!' said Holmes, bitterly, as he emerged panting and white with vexation from the tide of vehicles. 'Was ever such bad luck and such bad management, too? Watson, Watson, if you are an honest man you will record this also and set it against my successes!'

'Who was the man?'

'I have not an idea.'

7 DISCUSSION AND WRITING: A LEGEND

There are many actual legends in several parts of the country about spectral dogs that appear on misty nights. Which other local legends do you know? Discuss some as a class (including some of the modern 'urban myths') and use one of them in writing a mystery story.

8 WRITING: WHAT DO YOU THINK WILL HAPPEN TO STAPLETON?

Write a final scene for the play which makes his fate clear. Then compare your version with other people's.